Reader's Passages to Accompany
THE CRITICAL READING INVENTORY

Assessing Students' Reading and Thinking

SECOND EDITION

Mary DeKonty Applegate
St. Joseph's University

Kathleen Benson Quinn
Holy Family University

Anthony J. Applegate
Holy Family University

PEARSON
Merrill
Prentice Hall

Upper Saddle River, New Jersey
Columbus, Ohio

Vice President and Executive Publisher: Jeffery W. Johnston
Senior Editor: Linda Ashe Bishop
Senior Production Editor: Mary M. Irvin
Senior Editorial Assistant: Laura Weaver
Design Coordinator: Diane C. Lorenzo
Project Coordination: Carlisle Publishing Services
Cover Designer: Jeff Vanik
Cover Image: SuperStock
Production Manager: Pamela D. Bennett
Director of Marketing: David Gesell
Marketing Manager: Darcy Betts Prybella
Marketing Coordinator: Brian Mounts

The authors gratefully acknowledge the work of Walter J. Benson and Rob Ferguson for their illustrations in the pre-primary and primary reader's passages.

This book was set in Galliard by Carlisle Publishing Services. It was printed and bound by Courier/Kendallville, Inc. The cover was printed by Phoenix Color Corp.

Photo Credits: Kathleen Quinn, pp. 99, 100, 101, 102, 106, 107; Jason Edwards/National Geographic Image Collection, p. 104; Maria B. Vonada/Merrill, p. 105; Thomas Jenkins, Jr., pp. 111, 112; Richard Allen Wood/Animals Animals/Earth Scenes, p. 123.

Pearson Education Ltd.
Pearson Education Singapore Pte. Ltd.
Pearson Education Canada, Ltd.
Pearson Education–Japan

Pearson Education Australia Pty. Limited
Pearson Education North Asia Ltd.
Pearson Educación de Mexico, S.A. de C.V.
Pearson Education Malaysia Pte. Ltd.

10 9 8 7 6 5 4 3 2
ISBN-13: 978-0-13-158926-1
ISBN-10:   0-13-158926-1

Contents

Informational Passages 97

Word Lists

Word Lists

the	of
a	have
was	fig
he	day
go	came
boy	house
stop	play
come	little
and	saw
her	thing
dog	eat
book	wood
big	work
I	move
pet	just
cat	great
for	looked
sad	deep
do	happy
too	who

Word Lists

family	teacher
hear	clean
school	remember
hard	horse
feet	anyone
taken	birthday
fishing	garden
blue	street
before	guess
children	pretty
waited	fastest
puppy	against
every	animal
someone	excited
goods	laughing
found	together
cheese	camp
would	still
silly	finish
sorry	word

Word Lists

enter	doesn't
change	concern
lesson	sample
think	official
music	given
trust	present
human	decorate
pencil	windshield
mail	exercise
phone	finish
kitchen	science
interested	nothing
wildly	eager
breakfast	irritated
fence	clutter
toward	disappoint
season	range
nervous	dashed
caught	flown
wrong	chores

Word Lists

bravely	athletic
embarrass	psychology
importance	realize
guarantee	ridiculous
magical	successful
prevent	reluctant
typical	consideration
vision	mountainous
handle	partial
ledge	graceful
perhaps	several
province	incredible
decision	tutoring
breathing	fortunately
valuable	authors
disguise	conversations
muttered	self-pity
bounds	pronounce
toughest	calm
sprawled	mockingly

Word Lists

fundamental	jargon
humane	anticipate
siege	jeopardize
knuckle	calorie
assortment	diploma
exposure	financial
vital	heredity
waiver	logic
preference	plumage
biography	specific
newfound	sophisticated
intentions	utter
admiration	demolish
nuisance	pharmacies
resolution	chided
seasickness	savored
uncoordinated	competition
distract	interminable
mesmerized	edible
endeavor	cumbersome

Word Lists

administer	chagrin
nautical	granulate
squeamish	pinnacle
vestibule	mystical
bestow	demure
expenditure	stalwart
guidance	thermal
arbitrary	rhapsody
pennant	ethical
comparable	vitality
illustrious	startled
confident	grudgingly
intrigue	literally
anticipated	scrimped
troublesome	resplendent
pretext	unsavory
assurance	saliently
vividly	pathologist
curvature	waif
podium	hapless

Word Lists

amplitude	diminutive
luxuriant	impetuosity
fissure	candor
retina	recluse
guise	subterfuge
brevity	apparition
populace	parody
irrepressible	vulnerable
versatile	mediation
dispersion	fiscal
recruiters	sauntered
regrettable	acknowledged
consequential	cajoled
frantically	episodes
momentous	wheedled
captivated	benevolent
hysterically	regimen
nonchalantly	protégés
provocation	serenity
in absentia	propriety

Word Lists

to	fly
like	jump
am	went
get	skate
not	give
can	off
see	could
will	many
me	saw
you	out
pet	home
book	food
old	said
bake	some
at	away
be	rod
four	fast
my	took
bus	need
car	read

Word Lists

where	always
farm	walking
surprise	pull
friend	faster
drop	spring
won't	when
petting	help
made	know
bike	have
games	brother
bringing	daughter
asked	chance
ready	aunt
money	climbed
sleep	people
almost	their
picked	march
should	large
many	coach
heard	weekend

Word Lists

fright	enjoyable
unusual	wrong
they'll	quiet
bread	morning
forest	grandmother
early	huge
hurt	covered
water	thought
because	creature
hour	trouble
shouldn't	originality
barking	advice
faithful	sobbed
vacation	disgusted
roadside	rainspouts
championship	wondered
pitcher	length
trail	startled
hitting	afterwards
certain	grown-ups

Word Lists

wounded	applause
defend	survival
jungle	materials
seasonal	perplex
differently	license
through	vehicle
projection	definite
necessary	experience
medicine	predictable
mysterious	conform
marketplace	improve
participate	contribution
quitting	probably
calculate	difficulties
estimated	realized
pressured	occasion
teammates	mull
mocking	emerges
shoulder	impressed
disappointed	flinched

Word Lists

veneer	journalist
cavity	adequate
famine	browse
incredible	consistent
guardian	additional
relent	gill
version	investment
dialogue	masterpiece
longitude	resourceful
testimony	vouch
treasure	salon
prospect	murky
defiance	despised
excursion	emphatically
relieved	seethed
moaning	technique
prowess	combination
affection	jealousy
blurted	competition
unbelievably	binoculars

Word Lists

formidable	fraught
refinery	somber
audition	appropriation
sham	opaque
twinge	unerring
anecdote	plausible
destitute	bland
luminous	tolerable
inertia	wan
buffer	dynamic
trivial	ramshackle
incredulous	precinct
contracted	annoyance
luxury	inseparable
apprehensive	suppressed
muster	piqued
insistent	therapist
surmised	spontaneous
approximate	urchin
stunned	serene

Word Lists

complacent

populace

inherent

myriad

ruse

askew

socialist

procure

oscillate

exhilarated

engraved

wistfully

rehabilitation

reminisced

exasperation

confidantes

envisioned

vehemence

fatalistic

ophthalmologist

austerity

hieroglyphics

mundane

rhetoric

effervescence

predecessor

ostracize

corollary

subsidiary

guile

manipulative

exploits

whimpered

monumentally

indoctrination

tranquility

pessimism

idyllic

unalterably

diversity

Narrative Passages

At the Library

"I want a book.
I want a good book.
Please find a pet book for me," said the girl.

"Here is a cat book.
I can read you this cat book," said Mom.
"No, I do not like that book," said the girl.

"Here is a dog book.
I can read you this dog book," said Mom.
"No, I do not like that book," said the girl.

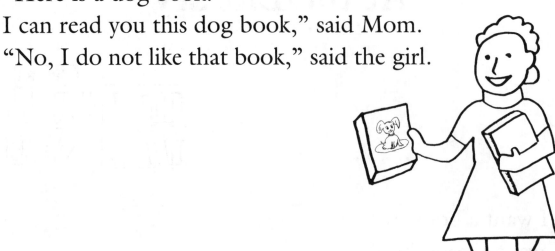

"What pet would you like to have?" asked Mom.
"I would like to have a bird," said the girl.
"That's a good pet," said Mom.
"Here is a bird book."

"Oh, I like that book.
"Please read me that book!"

The Baker

"Come in!" said the baker.
"I like to bake!
Look at the big cakes!
Look at the little cakes!"

"I want a big cake," said Jane.
"The cake is for my birthday party.
Four girls will come.
I will be four years old."

"I want a big cake," said Bill.
"The cake is for my birthday party.
Seven boys will come.
I will be seven years old."

"I want a big cake," said Mom.
"The cake is for my little girl.
She will be two years old.
We will have a party."

"I want the cake now," cried the little girl.
"I don't want a party."

"Look," said the baker.
"Here is a cupcake for you."

"Thank you!" said Mom.

No, No, Sue

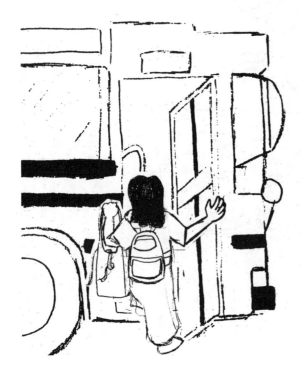

"Here comes the bus.
Get on the bus, Jane," said Mom.
"You have to go to school and read books."

"I want to go, too," said Sue.
"No, Sue. We have to go home," said Mom.
Sue was sad.

"Here comes your friend, Jane," said Mom.
"You can get in the car, Jane.
You worked hard at school.
You can go to the party."

"I want to go, too," said Sue.
"No, Sue. We have to stay home," said Mom.
Sue was very sad.
Mom was sad, too.

"We can go to the park now," said Mom.
"I have no more work to do."
"Good," said Sue.
Sue was happy.

"Here is the ride you like, Sue," said Mom.
"Get on the ride."
"Good," said Sue.
Sue was very happy.

The Little Fish

"Come Blue! Come Red!" said Mother Fish.

"Come, let's eat dinner."

Blue went to eat dinner.

Red saw a big fish come by and she chased the big fish away.

"Go away! This is our home!" said Red.

"What great food!" said Blue.

"Yes, this is good food," said Mother Fish. "Come and eat, Red."

But Red would not eat because she did not want to let the big fish come close.

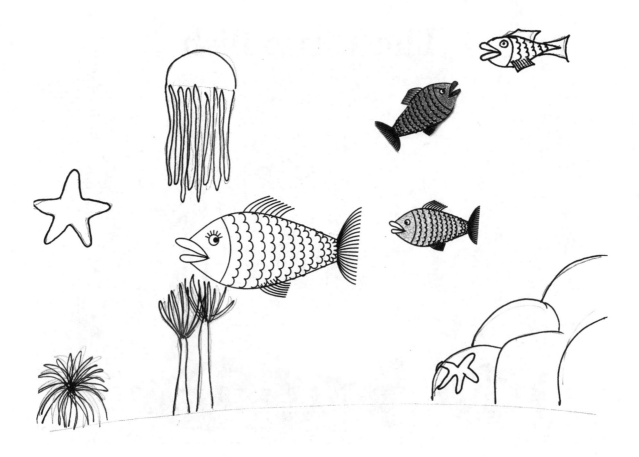

"Come Blue! Come Red!" said Mother Fish.

"Come, let's look at our pretty world."

Blue looked and looked.

Red saw a little fish come by and she chased the little
fish away.

"Go away! This is our home!" said Red.

"Come and look, Red," said Mother.

But Red would not look because she did not want to let
the little fish come close.

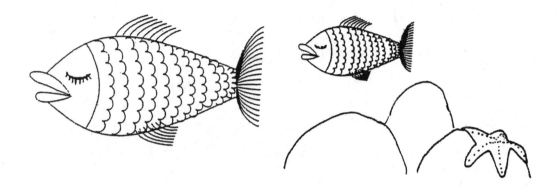

"Come Blue! Come Red!" said Mother Fish.

"We will have work to do tomorrow and we need to
    sleep."

Mother Fish fell asleep right away.

Blue fell asleep right away.

But Red could not sleep because she was still angry.

Learning to Fish

Pat said, "This is not fun!"

He was learning how to fish with his sister.

But the fish would not bite.

Pat jumped up. He shook the fishing rod.

He tried to get his bait closer to the fish.

Don't move the rod or you will scare the fish away,"
    said Dad.

Pat looked at his sister.

She had caught three fish already.

Then Pat threw some stones into the water.

You will scare the fish away," said Dad.

Pat was angry. He moved his rod and tried to make a
    fish take his bait.

This time Dad just watched.

Pat dropped his rod on the dock and walked away angry.

He sat on the shore and would not talk to his father or
    sister.

Just then a big fish took his bait.

Dad called, "Come quick! You've caught a fish!"

But Pat was not fast enough.

The fish pulled the whole rod into the deep water.

The Beaver Who Could Read

Chuck the beaver had a friend who was a squirrel.
The squirrel had books in his house.
He showed Chuck how to read.
Chuck learned quickly and he loved to read.

Chuck's father was not happy.
"Get to work, Chuck," said Dad.
"Beavers don't read. Beavers work.
We need a new house."

Chuck was sad because he wanted to read.
But Chuck went to work and he worked hard all day.
Then he saw a sign on a tree near the new house and he
    read the words.

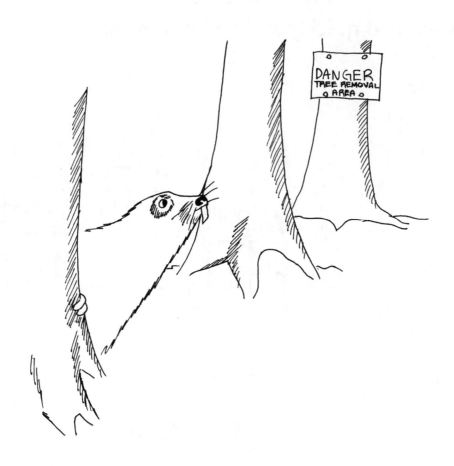

Chuck quickly ran home to Father.
"Father, we cannot build here.
I read the sign near our house.
People will come with big trucks and take all the trees
    away."

"I know the woods," said Father.

"I will say where our house will be."

But soon the trucks came and Father saw that they
could not build there.

"I was wrong, Son," said Father.

"You saved us by reading.

I am proud of you."

Chuck smiled a huge smile.

"Son, do you think you can teach me, too?"

Chuck smiled an even bigger smile.

Where Is the Dog?

Jan waited at the door. She was waiting for the car to come. Aunt Sara was coming for a visit and she was bringing Sally. Jan loved to play with Sally and she loved Aunt Sara, too.

"Here they are!" Jan called to Mother. Jan ran outside to meet Sally and Aunt Sara.

"Look what I have," said Sally. Sally showed Jan her little white puppy.

"Can I hold the puppy?" asked Jan.

"Oh, yes," said Sally.

Sally took the puppy into the house. Jan and Sally played with the puppy. Then they read books and played games. They had fun.

Then Sally went to help her mother. Jan played with the puppy. After lunch, Sally looked for her puppy. She looked and looked but she could not find her.

Aunt Sara and Mother helped her look. They asked Jan to help find the puppy.

"She is outside," said Jan.

"How did she get out?" asked Mother.

"She wanted to go out," said Jan.

"So I let her go."

Aunt Sara and Mother ran outside. Everyone looked and looked for the puppy. Jan was afraid.

Then Sally saw the puppy sitting under a car. Everyone was happy!

"You can not let the dog go out," said Aunt Sara. "She is too young. She will get lost."

The Pigs Get a Job

Father Pig had a big apple farm.

He had two sons.

Their names were Pete and Jake.

They worked every day with Father.

Soon Pete and Jake got older.

They were ready to leave home.

Pete bought an apple farm.

Pete said, "I worked for Father every day.

We worked so hard.

I will find a little dog to work for me.

He will work hard."

Pete found a little dog to work for him.

The little dog worked hard.

But Pete wanted more apples.

He told the little dog to work harder.

The little dog came to work early.

The dog picked more apples but he was always tired.

The dog did not like his job.

Jake bought an apple farm.

Jake said, "I worked with Father every day.

We had lots of fun working together.

I will find a little cat to work with me."

So Jake asked a little cat to work with him.

Jake and the cat worked together every day.

Jake said, "You can keep the extra apples we pick."

The little cat came to work early.

She took apples home for her mother.

She worked hard but she was happy.

The Cheese Factory

Flip and Buzz lived in Mouse Land and worked at the Cheese Factory.

One day they went to work but there was no cheese in the factory.

"Where is all the cheese?" they asked.

They went to see Wise Old Mouse.

He said, "Go see the dogs and they will help you find the cheese."

Flip was very angry. "The dogs were our friends," she said. "Why would they take our cheese?"

"Wise Old Mouse did not say that the dogs took our cheese," said Buzz.

Flip and Buzz went to see the dogs and they asked the first dog that they saw, "Do you know where our cheese is?"

"Go to your factory," said the dog.

"This is silly," said Flip. "We just came from the factory."

"I know," said Buzz. "But the dog sounded as if he knows something."

On the way to the factory, they saw many dogs carrying cheese.

"What are you doing with our cheese?" asked Buzz.

"We heard the rats saying that they were going to steal your cheese. We did not have time to tell you so we hid all the cheese before they got there. Then we waited for the rats. We told them no one works here anymore and they went away."

"I'm very sorry," said Flip. "You really are our friends after all."

The Race

Spencer was the fastest animal in the jungle. All of the other animals knew it. Spencer made sure of that. He would say, "No one can beat me! You are all too afraid to race!" It was true. No one wanted to race against Spencer. He always won. Then he would brag even more.

One day another family of cats moved in. Spencer ran up to the new family. He said, "I'm the fastest animal in the jungle. Do you want to race?" The father said, "No, thank you. But maybe our daughter Annie will race with you." Annie smiled and said, "Yes. I'd love to race." Soon the two cats were running for the finish line. Spencer was winning as always. But Annie was very fast. She raced past him and crossed the finish line first.

The other animals cheered in surprise. But Spencer cried, "I want another chance!" They raced again and again. But the result was still the same. There was a new champion in the jungle and her name was Annie.

All the animals came over to talk to Annie. But Spencer went away angry. Annie was a little sad. She hoped that Spencer would be her friend. "Well, at least we won't have to listen to him brag again," said the fox. The next day Spencer was back. The first thing he said was, "I can jump higher than anybody in the jungle! No one can beat me!" The other animals groaned and rolled their eyes. Nothing had changed after all.

The Roller Coaster Ride

Today it was finally Jessie's birthday. She jumped out of bed and called to her mom. "Mom, can you come here and see how tall I am?" She ran to the wall and waited. Mother marked the spot where Jessie had grown since her last birthday. "I made it!" shouted Jessie. "I'm tall enough to ride the roller coaster now!" On Saturday, Jessie, her mom, and Aunt Jane would go to the park. Then she could take her first ride!

Mom was too afraid to ride so Aunt Jane took Jessie to the line to wait their turn. Jessie and Aunt Jane jumped into a car and pulled the bar over their heads. Then they waited for the ride to start. "Let's get going," thought Jessie. Soon the ride started and Jessie was really excited. She felt very grown up. Then the car climbed higher and higher. It came down and went faster and faster. Jessie was so afraid that she thought she was going to die.

Jessie held Aunt Jane's arm. She covered her face and screamed. Jessie prayed that the ride would end. "Don't let me die," she prayed, "and I'll never ride a roller coaster again." Aunt Jane hugged Jessie. Jessie opened her eyes and she saw people laughing and screaming. Aunt Jane was laughing, too. They were all having fun.

The car slowed and then stopped. The ride was finally over. "Aunt Jane," said Jessie, "can we do it again?"

Keeping Your Word

"You made me sell candy bars all day Saturday," cried Steve to Dad.

"I didn't make you do it," said Dad. "The coach said your team could win a weekend at camp. You gave your word when you said that you would sell candy."

"But Rod didn't sell candy. His father took him swimming all day," said Steve.

"I know," said Dad. "But you kept your word and that's what counts."

The next Saturday Dad took Steve to the food market. Steve worked for four hours and he sold lots of candy bars but he still had many more left to sell. He was very angry when he came home on Monday. "Rod's father took him swimming again!" he said.

This time his father said, "What counts is what you do! I am very proud that you decided to keep your word and it is important that you are proud, too."

In the next two weeks Steve sold all of his candy bars and then the coach called the team together. "I have good news," he said. "We made enough money so that everyone on the team can go to camp."

Steve went to the weekend camp with his team and watched as Rod fished and played ping-pong. Steve did the same things, but he did not have fun.

When Steve came home, he asked his Father, "Why did they let Rod go to camp?" Dad said, "I don't think that was right but I didn't make the rules. I hope that you did not let your anger keep *you* from having a great time." Steve thought about what his father said and did not answer.

The Farm Vacation

It was five o'clock in the morning when David heard his grandfather call. David never got up this early before but he didn't mind at all! He was visiting his grandfather's farm for the first time and he was excited. He had always wanted to be a farmer and now he would have his chance. Besides, Grandpa had horses too and David looked forward to learning how to ride.

When David ran into the kitchen, Grandfather said, "Eat a good breakfast, Dave. We've got a lot to do this morning. We'll start with the hay."

"Don't rush him!" said Grandma. "Are you sure you want to work with Grandpa all day?" she asked David.

"Sure am!" said David. He gulped down his breakfast and dashed out to help load the hay wagon. He never knew hay was so heavy.

"You finish up here while I get the tractor. We've got some work to do in the garden," said Grandpa.

David walked over to the garden and climbed on to the tractor. Up and down they drove, row after row, turning up the soil as they went. "Lunch time," said Grandpa when the sun was overhead.

"When do the horses get fed?" David asked Grandma as he walked into the kitchen.

"Do you want to do that after lunch? You've worked so much already," said Grandma.

"Don't forget, honey," said Grandpa, "we've got lots to do. That's how life is on the farm."

"That's OK," said David. "Maybe I better stay and help Grandpa."

After lunch, David worked under the hot sun, helping Grandpa dig postholes for a new fence. Then David and Grandpa picked corn and brought it to their roadside stand. David was trudging slowly back toward the house when Grandma called, "Do you want to feed the horses?"

David ran to the barn and helped to feed the horses. "I wish I could ride you," he said to each one as he rubbed its nose. "Maybe Grandpa will teach me!"

David fell asleep immediately that night but when the sun rose the next morning, he was not so eager to get up. He had the feeling that today would be another day just like yesterday. As it turned out, he was right.

"Do you still want to be a farmer?" asked Grandfather at the end of the week. "I'm not so sure," David replied. "If the sun rose at ten o'clock and there wasn't so much hard work, then maybe farming would be more fun."

The Championship Game

At the end of a long softball season, Jill's team made it to the championship game. They would play against the top team in the league, the Ramblers. Before the game, the teams practiced throwing and catching the ball. As Jill watched her teammates, she knew that they would have a hard time winning. Three of the girls kept dropping the ball during practice and the team's best pitcher was as awful as Jill had ever seen her. Jill thought that if her team was going to win, she would have to be the one to get the job done. Soon the coach called the players in to sing the national anthem. Jill thought to herself, "This is just like it will be when I get to the pros." She knew the other players were nervous, but not her! She couldn't wait to start the game.

Early in the game, Jill's team took a 1–0 lead. Jill came up to bat with a runner on second base, but when she didn't swing at the ball, the umpire called "Strike three!" She couldn't believe that he would call such a terrible pitch a strike. She really wanted to say to him, "You just called strike three on Jill, the best player on the team." By the third inning, Jill's team was ahead 3–0 and the team was looking good. But Jill still didn't have a hit. Her next time up, she hit the ball a long way and when the ball was caught, she blamed a gust of wind for taking away her home run.

Then the Ramblers scored four runs and took the lead. Soon Jill had her chance to be the star. Her team had two players on base but Jill had two strikes on her. Then she got the pitch she was looking for and she swung with all her might. She couldn't believe that she missed it. Jill sat down, angry that the sun had gotten in her eyes at the wrong time. She just couldn't see the ball. The next player up hit the ball to left field and scored the two runs that the team needed. When the game ended, Jill's team had won 5–4. The team went wild, but Jill didn't feel like celebrating. Even after the team picture, Jill felt terrible. It was her worst game all season and it was the biggest game of the season, too. She wished that she had done better in front of all those people.

Boy's Best Friend

Todd ran down to the kitchen and shouted, "Check out this team jacket!" As soon as he heard Todd, Dusty came running and jumped up, trying to lick Todd's face. "Get down right now!" cried Todd. "You'll mess up my new jacket!"

"He's so happy to see you," said Mom. "You shouldn't yell at him. Don't forget, a dog is man's best friend."

But Todd wasn't very interested in Dusty because he was thinking about the mountain bike race next week. This was a special race for third graders and his team really wanted to win. He would be the first rider on his team and he knew he would have to give his team a big lead.

"I have to go and practice. I need to be the fastest rider." Dusty couldn't wait either and he dashed out the door to follow Todd up to the hill. "Keep Dusty at home," Todd called to his mother, but Mother was so interested in making sure that Todd wore his helmet that she forgot to call Dusty.

Todd rode faster and faster as he rode down the bike trail. He knew the course like the back of his hand but knowing the course so well was not enough. Todd went too fast and never saw the rock that he hit with his front wheel. The last thing he remembered was hitting the ground hard.

When Dusty caught up with Todd, he started barking. He wanted Todd to get up and walk but when Todd did not move, Dusty turned suddenly and ran back home.

Mom had a feeling that something was wrong when she heard Dusty barking so wildly. When she ran out of the house and saw Dusty without Todd, she was certain that something was wrong. She quickly called the firehouse for help.

Dusty faced the hill, barking until help came. He ran off before Mom had the chance to say "Find Todd." Mom and the firemen followed Dusty to Todd and then took him to the hospital. Dusty waited in the truck with Todd's broken helmet.

Todd soon woke up and started to talk. The doctor told Todd's mother and father that Todd would be fine. "The helmet took most of the force of his fall," said the doctor. "He was very fortunate that he was wearing it." Todd would only need to rest, but he would not be able to ride for at least a month. Todd was in bed that night when Dusty came into his room. Todd hugged his faithful dog. "Mom is right," said Todd. "A dog is a boy's best friend!"

The Vacation

Juan burst into his sister's room. "Only eight more days!" he shouted.

"I started packing already!" said Maria. "I can't wait to see what Florida is like."

Juan and Maria had started every day for the last two weeks talking about their Florida vacation. Mom and Dad were just as eager as they were.

But that evening, Father walked into the house, looking like a ghost. "What's wrong?" Mother asked.

"No more overtime for the rest of the year," he stammered. Mother knew that they were going to use the overtime money to pay for the hotel rooms and the plane tickets to Florida. This was their first family vacation!

Mr. Ruiz struggled as he told the children that they would have to cancel their vacation. Juan ran up to his room crying while Maria hugged her father and sobbed.

"Let me see what I can do," said Mrs. Ruiz as she left the room.

She was smiling from ear to ear when she returned. "I just spoke with my brother Sal and he said that we could use his van to drive to Florida and we can stay with his wife's sister!"

Maria was excited with the news but Juan was angry! That wasn't the fun vacation he had been dreaming of for weeks. He had never flown on an airplane and he had never stayed in a hotel.

During the trip, the family stopped to look at different sights along the way. But every time Juan refused to leave the van. He was irritated with their jabbering about what they had seen at each stop.

The following day, Juan again sat in the van while the others went out to see a nearby river. Suddenly, Maria came rushing back to the van. "Juan! Juan!" she called, "Hurry, there's an alligator!" Juan jumped out of the van and dashed the quarter mile to where his parents were standing.

"You missed it," said his father sadly. "It's gone!"

Maria, Mom, and Dad told Juan how they first saw the alligator sunning itself on the bank of the river. Maria had quietly run back to get Juan but a squawking bird startled the alligator and it dashed into the river.

Everyone saw how disgusted Juan was and no one said a word for over twenty minutes.

"You know, Juan . . ." began Mother.

"I know, Mom," said Juan. "I've been missing one of the best chances I've ever had! But I won't do it again!"

Autumn Leaves

"Libby, come here quick," I called. "The leaves are all falling." It is fall and my little sister, Libby, and I will have to rake the leaves together every day. Mom said that Libby is finally old enough to help with the chores and that I have the job of showing her how to clean up the yard. If we don't rake up the leaves, they will clutter up the lawn, the sidewalks, and even the rainspouts. Mom says that falling leaves are messy and dangerous, especially when they are wet.

"Look at all the leaves, Sue!" shouted Libby. "I want to go out and play right now!" I told her that we couldn't play just then. "Mom wants us to rake the leaves up. If it rains, people walking by our house might slip and fall."

"Please, Sue. Let's just jump in them for a little while," she begged. So I told her that if she would help me clean up afterwards, we could pile them up into a big mound and jump in. She was so excited that she promised to help me.

"We went out and raked the leaves into a big pile and then we shouted "one, two, three, jump!" And we jumped on the pile of leaves again and again until the leaves were scattered over the entire yard. Then I told Libby that it was time to rake them up, but Libby just wanted to keep playing. While she played, I had to gather the leaves and put them in the trash bags myself. Then I had to drag all of the bags out to the sidewalk for the trucks to come and pick them up the next morning. I knew that more leaves would fall tomorrow but I wondered if Libby would help me clean them up then.

The next day, I had piano lessons so I didn't get home until late. I was surprised to find that Libby had gone outside and raked the leaves herself. But then she remembered the fun she had the day before and she jumped in them and they flew all over the yard. When I saw the mess I told Libby that she would have to clean up the leaves. I even offered to help her rake them up before Mom came home. But Libby ran away to play with her friend and I was left to do all of the work again. I really wanted to just leave everything there in the yard but I knew that Mom would be disappointed. Falling leaves can be fun for kids, but grown-ups don't see it that way. I think I'm starting to see the reason.

The Science Fair

"It is time for the Science Fair," said Mr. Jones. "You should pick something you want to learn about and make sure it is important to you." As soon as Mr. Jones talked about the Science Fair, everyone turned to look at Ben. That was no surprise because Ben had won the first prize last year. He had created an original computer game and his friends loved playing it. No other project in the fair was even close to his.

Ben saw everyone looking at him but he knew down deep that he had lots of help last year. In fact, his father did most of the work. Many times there was nothing for Ben to do and so he went and watched TV. "What will I do this year?" thought Ben. He knew that he was in trouble because his dad had a new job. "He will be away for two months and so this time I will have to make something by myself," he thought.

Ben thought about his problem for many days. He had no idea what he could do but then he remembered Mr. Jones's advice. "This time I am going to do something that I really like even if it isn't great," he thought.

Ben thought about what he loved to do most and that was to play golf with his father. But when he played, he could never hit the ball far. Ben decided that he would learn how to make golf balls fly. He went to the library and found three books on golf. He read the books and made a chart to show what he learned.

Ben went to the golf range three times every week, trying hard to follow the advice from the books. He kept his eyes on the ball and tried not to swing too hard. After each try he charted the length of his drives, keeping a graph that showed how he did every day.

Everyone was surprised when Ben came to the fair with nothing but a simple chart and a graph that plotted his progress. Ben was really proud of the growth he had made. He was disappointed when no one said anything about his hard work or his creativity. His father called that weekend and Ben told him that he was not very happy with the low grade he had received on the science project. "But I did just what Mr. Jones said we were to do. I learned about something that was really important to *me*."

Getting What You Want

Many years ago a young woman named Winnie Yua lived in a small Chinese village where her family kept a few rice paddies. Winnie's family was very poor. Winnie was the oldest of five girls and she would help her father take the rice to the city and sell it on market days. Her parents had always hoped to have a son who would be able to go to school and perhaps work in the city for better pay. They never had their son, but their daughters were all good and kind and worked hard on the farm with their parents.

One day in the marketplace, Winnie heard news from the province that the emperor had announced a counting contest. This was exciting news because the winner would get a valuable, secret prize. Winnie knew no one who was nearly as good at counting as she was. But when she asked about how to enter the contest, Winnie learned that only boys were permitted to participate.

"Father, I wish I were a boy. I know that I can count very well. It isn't fair that only boys can compete."

"Winnie, you really need to stop wishing you were a boy. Sometimes I think it is our fault that you feel that way. You are a good daughter and a great help to us. I know it isn't fair that the emperor is only allowing boys to participate but that is the way it is. Perhaps one day things will change but you must accept your fate for now."

Winnie honored and respected her father, but she still wanted a chance to win a valuable prize and help her family. Helping at the market had made her an excellent counter. She could calculate bills and change without an abacus. And she never made a mistake. So Winnie vowed to win the prize and immediately set out to make for herself a special suit of boy's clothing. On the day of the competition, Winnie disguised herself as a young man and entered the contest. As the day went on, Winnie became more and more excited. The others were failing, one by one, but Winnie knew her numbers well. At the end of the contest, she was the only one left. She had achieved her goal!

Now the emperor's minister came forward to award the prize. Winnie's heart was pounding. It seemed as if everyone in the entire city was there to hear the announcement. She prayed that no one would recognize her. All she wanted was to take the money, go home to her own village, and surprise her family, especially her father.

Then the crowd hushed at a signal from the town's guard. Then the minister spoke in a loud voice, "The emperor has decreed that the winner of this contest is the man who will marry his only daughter!"

The Player

Rasheed was excited to be playing on his first basketball team. He hadn't played much basketball but he had always been big and fast and a good athlete. But this time things were different. The first time he had the ball, Rasheed dribbled it off his foot and out of bounds. The next two times, a quicker player stole it away from him. Finally Rasheed had his first chance to shoot the ball but he missed everything, even the backboard. Soon his teammates stopped passing the ball to him, even when he was open under the basket. His team lost the game badly and Rasheed went home angry with his team and angry with basketball.

That night, Rasheed went to his father and told him that he wanted to quit the basketball team. "I'm no good at basketball and the team is no good either," he said.

"Well, if you want to quit, that's your decision," said Mr. Singer. "But I think if you really want to, you can become a whole lot better and so can your team. Maybe you shouldn't just do things that are easy for you." Rasheed had to think this one over. Rasheed knew that whenever his father said "It's your decision, but . . ." he really meant that he'd like Rasheed to think it over very carefully. Down deep, he knew that his father would be disappointed if he never even tried to become a better player.

Rasheed knew that his father wouldn't be much help at teaching him basketball but he had heard stories about their new neighbor, Mr. Armstrong, being named to the all-state team in high school. When Rasheed asked Mr. Armstrong if he could teach him basketball, Mr. Armstrong's eyes lit up. He said, "You stick with me, kid, and you'll be the best basketball player ever!" Rasheed laughed as the two of them took turns shooting baskets in Mr. Armstrong's back yard. But soon Rasheed was sweating and breathing hard as his new teacher put him through one basketball drill after another. Finally, Mr. Armstrong said, "Time to call it a day! But be here same time tomorrow and we'll do it again." Rasheed worked hard and even after just a few days, he could feel himself becoming more confident in his ability. When it was time for the next game, Rasheed scored eight points, grabbed five rebounds, and didn't lose the ball once. His team still lost the game, but his teammates couldn't believe how much better he had become.

After the game, Mr. Singer put his arm around his son and said, "I'm really proud of the decision you made, Rasheed. You worked awfully hard and it really showed."

"Thanks, Dad. Thanks for not letting me quit the team."

"Who told you that you couldn't quit? It wasn't me!"

Rasheed just smiled.

The Bully

Bill overheard his father talking to Chip's dad, "I'm sure you're proud of how Chip hits the ball." Bill knew that his father admired Chip's athletic skills. "That Chip is really a special kid," his father said, and he said it more often than Bill cared to remember.

"How come you don't spend more time with Chip?" his father asked. "I spend a lot of time with him," said Bill, hoping his father didn't hear the discomfort in his voice. He didn't want to admit that he didn't like Chip at all.

Earlier that same afternoon Bill had been walking with his friend Pedro when Chip turned the corner and saw them. He called out, "Hey Pedro, why don't you learn to talk like a *real* American? If you did, you could help your father talk so people can understand him." Chip laughed loudly and walked off still laughing. This kind of insult was nothing new for Chip, but what really annoyed Bill was that Chip never acted this way in front of adults. But when he was alone with classmates, he had a way of finding their weak spots and making fun of them in front of their friends.

Pedro didn't want Bill to know he was hurt, so he muttered something about having work to do and ran off as fast as he could. Bill wanted to tell Chip where to get off but that might just start a fight. And Chip was too big and strong for Bill to take on.

The next day, Bill was on his way to Pedro's house so Pedro could help him with his math homework. As he turned the corner, he saw Chip and another boy pushing Pedro down on the grass and making fun of him. "Dat' eees not white!" they said, mocking the way Pedro talked. "Don't you even know how to say *right* the right way?"

"Let him alone," shouted Bill, so angry that he didn't care that he was standing up to the two toughest kids in the class. Bill marched right up to Chip's face shouting, "You'd better cut it out now!" Before Bill knew what had happened, Chip had knocked him on the ground, right next to Pedro. Bill never expected to see Pedro jump up and run right into Chip, and he never expected to see Chip sprawled out on the ground. Bill leaped up to his feet and stood shoulder to shoulder with Pedro. He was really surprised when Chip and his friend, seeing how angry Pedro and Bill were, decided to back off and walk quickly away.

Bill decided that it was finally time to tell his father about Chip. "I was always afraid to say anything because I knew how much you liked him," Bill said. His father replied, "I'm sorry, Bill. I should have never pressured you to be his friend. The Chip I liked doesn't really exist!"

The Motor Bike

Vic sprinted down the street knowing that Jameer would be waiting for him. For the past several months they had been meeting with Mr. Hunter before school started to discuss the books they were reading. On the way, Vic's mind wandered back to his third grade teacher, Ms. Woodson, and how she had changed his way of thinking. She helped him see that reading and learning could help people improve their lives.

"Guess what?" hollered Jameer when Vic was still a distance away. "I'm getting that incredible motor for my bike that I've been telling you about. Everybody in the family gets something special for their sixteenth birthday and this is my special gift!" Vic was happy for his old friend but he couldn't help feeling just a little envious too. He really wished that he had something exceptional to look forward to on his birthday.

Mr. Hunter started class and the book discussion turned toward the influences and contributions of parents to the lives of authors. Vic realized with a growing sense of discomfort that he had absolutely nothing to add to the conversation. How could he tell them that he hardly ever saw his mother, that she had two jobs and that he was the one who had to supervise his brothers and sisters? By the end of the class, his self-pity was overflowing. Mr. Hunter walked out with Vic at the end of class and said, "My wife and I would like you to have dinner with us next Saturday. See if it's OK for you."

Vic spent the following Saturday evening with the Hunter family. After dinner, Mrs. Hunter sat with Vic and showed him photographs from her childhood. In her entire collection, she had only three photographs of her mother but when Mrs. Hunter got to the first one, her face softened. She told Vic how her mother had worked at two jobs from day to night to be sure that her children always had clothes and food. "This picture was taken shortly before she died," she said. "That was the first time I told her that I resented the fact that she had missed practically every important occasion in my life. That's when she showed me her album. She kept photos and clippings from every one of those events that she had missed because she couldn't take time off from her job. Some people can't express their love with words but they certainly can show it. We just have to have enough insight to read it."

Vic had a lot to mull over that weekend and the next day he called Mrs. Hunter and said, "You know, I learned about reading from Ms. Woodson but she never taught me about the different kinds of reading; I guess we have to read things besides books. I think I'm going to try to get better at reading people. Maybe I've been getting special gifts, just like Jameer, but I never even knew it. Thanks."

The Tutor

Jack went to his room very troubled; tomorrow he had to begin participating in the school's tutoring program. As he lay in bed, all the embarrassing reading experiences from grade school bombarded his mind. He remembered having to read aloud in front of the class, stumbling over the words he couldn't pronounce. Now he had to spend one period each day in the second grade class, helping a younger student who was having problems reading. "I'll probably end up making him feel worse than I used to feel!" he thought.

"You'll really enjoy it," said Ms. Anderson, his homeroom teacher, trying to calm Jack as he reluctantly left for his tutoring assignment the following day. "All you have to do is let your student select a book, read it to him, and then discuss it with him. Just ask him to look for different ways that the story had something to do with his life."

Jack hoped that Carl, the little boy to whom he was assigned, wouldn't notice how uncomfortable he felt reading with him. Fortunately, Carl selected a story that Jack had no difficulty reading and one that had an interesting twist, too. The story, *An Extraordinary Egg,* was about a frog who discovered a large egg which her sister, with complete confidence, identified as a chicken egg. When the egg hatches and an alligator emerges, the frogs continue to call it a chicken throughout the entire story. Carl laughed out loud as Jack read the story; in fact, Jack couldn't help laughing with him.

"The one frog was a real know-it-all," said Carl. "My friend Bob is just the same way because he tries to make me feel stupid. Just because he's a good reader doesn't mean that he knows everything! Do you have any know-it-all friends?"

"Quite a few," said Jack. "When they talk, they act conceited. They try to convince other people that they're great." He was impressed with Carl's insight into his friend and how he used Carl's reading difficulties as a justification to put him down.

"That's exactly what the frog in the story did too," said Carl. "She even laughed at the mother alligator for calling the creature an alligator and not a chicken. Really, somebody should have laughed at her!" Jack suddenly remembered the times that certain of his classmates had laughed at him. "Do you think laughing at people is a very good way to get them to change?" "I guess that probably wouldn't work," said Carl.

"I feel sorry for the frog who was always exploring and discovering things, but nobody at home ever got excited with her. My parents always get excited when I do anything. I think that they want me to feel smart even though I'm not a good reader. You probably never had to worry about that when you were in second grade."

"You can never really know for sure about things like that. Maybe we should talk about school experiences next time."

The Dentist

Bob bit his lip, trying hard to forget his throbbing toothache as he ran to his friend's home. He had finally become the band's official drummer and no toothache was going to stop him from playing. In spite of his pain, Bob never flinched, making sure no one knew as he concentrated on keeping his drum rolls in rhythm. As he made his way home, the pain in his tooth seemed to become more intense with every step.

"Mom, how can you just let me hurt like this?" he cried as he walked in the door, ran into his bedroom, threw himself on the bed, and sobbed. Mother rushed into the room in a panic and asked, "What's wrong?" "I can't take this pain in my tooth!" Bob cried. "I didn't even know!" his mother exclaimed, as she scurried off to phone their dentist.

When she left, Bob's older sister, Stella, stood at the door muttering, "You are such a baby, making a mountain out of a mole hill!" Bob cried back, "Anybody who had a toothache like this would be crying!" Stella snapped back, "Were you crying like that when you were playing in the band this morning?"

Mother returned with the news that their dentist could see Bob the following morning, and just the knowledge that the problem would be solved, coupled with a few aspirin, was enough to relieve Bob and he headed off to watch television. When Bob left, his sister turned to Mother and said haughtily, "He's such a baby and you're not doing anything to stop it. Isn't it really interesting that he only cries around us?" "Are you forgetting that home is our comfort zone?" said Mother.

The next morning as Bob and his mother drove to the dentist, Bob remained silent for most of the ride. As they neared the dentist's office, he blurted, "Mom, when the nurse asks me if I want you to come back with me to the dentist's chair, I'm going to say 'no' but make sure you come back with me anyway!" Mother smiled, thinking to herself what Stella would be saying if she had heard that. Just as directed, Mother went with Bob after he told the nurse that he didn't need her. On the way home, a pain-free Bob chatted about the funny things the dentist had said and then, smiling, he said, "Mom, when we go back tomorrow and I say you don't have to come back, you *really* don't."

At home, Stella asked mockingly, "You mean you're really going to survive?" Mom waited until Bob left and then asked, "Why are you so hard on him? I remember when you were young and you reacted exactly the same way whenever you had an earache. You'll find that it's time that helps us grow up. Bob is well on his way!"

The Pet

Linda was walking through the woods near her home as she so often did during the summer. All of a sudden she spied a beautifully colored garden snake, slithering among the dried blades of grass. "What an awesome pet that would make!" thought Linda as she scrambled to capture the hapless snake. "My friends will just die when I show them this! Not one of them would have the courage to keep a snake as a pet!"

Linda hurried home to display her newfound treasure to her mother. Somehow she wasn't surprised with her mother's less than enthusiastic reaction to a garden snake as a household pet. "You haven't the slightest idea how to feed or to take care of that animal," said Mom. "If you really wanted to do the right thing, you'd take him right back to where you found him and let him go free."

But Linda had no intentions whatsoever of losing her prize or of giving up the prospect of her friends' admiration and awe. It took quite some time, but she finally convinced her mother that she would learn how to feed the snake and take care of its needs. Although Mother knew her daughter very well, she still agreed to allow Linda to keep the snake, on the condition that Linda would do her research and learn what she needed to know. "Well, who knows? Maybe this time things will be different," thought Mother, as she went about her business feeling disappointed with herself.

The rest of the story is very predictable. Linda's pet elicited the responses she had hoped for from her friends: they were both impressed with and jealous of her exotic pet. But when the novelty wore off and the snake no longer excited the curiosity of her peers, Linda was disappointed. "These people are so picky that nothing keeps them interested!" she told herself on the way home. Then on top of it all, she had to listen to her mother's incessant nagging, "You can't just give the snake scraps of table food when you see that he isn't eating them. He's getting weaker every day, so why don't you for once do the right thing and let him go?" said Mother, unable to hide her irritation.

Linda knew full well that the consequences of outright defiance would be severe, so she simply turned a deaf ear on her mother's complaints. The next day she returned to find that the converted bird cage that she kept the snake in was empty. Running to her mother's room, she demanded to know what had happened to her snake. "You didn't take care of him and you wouldn't do the right thing, so I did it for you," said Mother. "I took the snake back to where he belongs." Linda bolted out of the house furious, muttering to herself that one day she would tell her mother exactly what was on her mind. "She never lets me live my own life the way that I want to live it!" Many days would pass before life in Linda's house settled back to normal.

The Fishing Trip

Rick could hardly wait for the end of August when his favorite uncle had planned to treat him to his first deep-sea fishing excursion. Rick would finally be angling for really big fish and not just casting for trout! The only dark side to the trip was that his older brother would be going too. Kent was three years his senior and could be a serious nuisance with his nonstop teasing, but Rick was resolved not to let an annoying brother wreck his plans for a fantastic fishing trip.

When the grand day finally arrived, Rick and Kent enthusiastically greeted their Uncle John at the dock. Rick was more than a little relieved to see that their cruiser was both spacious and substantial. "Hope you don't get seasick, squirt," laughed Kent, but Rick remembered his resolution and simply ignored his brother. When the boat finally departed the dock and headed out to deeper water, Rick was spellbound for what seemed like an eternity by the sheer power and beauty of the ocean. He was snapped out of his reverie by the sound of his uncle's voice, reminding the boys to get their fishing gear in order. That's when he first noticed Kent, unsteady on his feet and rapidly turning a sickly shade of green.

Fortunately, Uncle John knew all the signs of impending seasickness and quickly scooped Kent up and carried him below to the boat's lower cabin. The cabin was poorly lit, grimy, and smelled of diesel fumes but Uncle John found Kent a place on one of the wooden benches that lined the cabin, wrapped him in a blanket, and told him to rest as best he could. "There isn't much that we can do until we can get Kent back, so you might as well come up and fish, Rick," he said. When he heard his uncle's words, Kent's eyes widened and he stared desperately at his brother. Rick realized that if the shoe were on the other foot he would be terrified to be left in the cabin alone. Still, he couldn't help thinking that his brother would rather die than admit it.

"That's OK, Uncle John. Maybe I should just stay for a while with Kent." Rick sat for what seemed like hours, with his brother alternating between fitful naps and periods of moaning. Rick couldn't help but feel angry with Kent for ruining his trip, but at the same time, he had never seen his brother quite so sick and helpless. All in all, Rick had the feeling that he was doing the right thing.

By the time Kent began to recover enough to sit up, the boat was already powering back toward the dock. "I don't know why you didn't go and fish with Uncle John, you little jerk," said Kent. "I didn't need you to stay with me. I'd have been fine by myself." Rick turned away hastily so that Kent wouldn't see the anger in his face. It wasn't until years later that the brothers would realize what good friends they had always been.

Brother's Letter

It was close to midnight and Luke still wanted to talk. Chad waited patiently, knowing how much his little brother would miss him when he departed the next morning for hockey camp. Chad was a star athlete but Luke, in spite of all of his efforts, was an uncoordinated bookworm with no athletic prowess and few friends, and Chad was more than a little worried about him.

Although Gramps had died several years before his brother was born, Luke had always been fascinated by the stories that Chad told him, so Chad thought that perhaps a few tales of Gramps would distract him. "I really wish you had a chance to know Gramps," began Chad. "Gramps used to write stories and read them to me. His favorites were the ones where he would get inside someone's head and try to see things the way that other person would see them. He told me that if I could do that, it would help me in sports and he was right."

"I always wondered why Gramps didn't become a writer," said Luke.

"When he was in high school he liked writing stories but nobody paid much attention. He knew his family didn't have the money to send him to college so he just wrote for himself."

"Do you think you have lots of friends because you're good in sports?" asked Luke, catching Chad off guard. "No," Chad lied, "I have lots of friends because I try to be myself." "That doesn't work for me," replied Luke, as he began to drift off to sleep.

Early the following week, Chad received a letter from his brother and was overjoyed to hear that Luke had found a new friend. "My friend loves handball and I tried to play but I felt like a failure, and then I sort of did what Gramps said and I made up a story. But in the story I was my friend instead of me so I'd like you to read it and tell me what you think." Chad steeled himself for a lengthy bout of boredom, but he found himself pleasantly surprised. Luke was a very accomplished writer for his age, and he seemed to have the knack of being able to walk in the shoes of other people. Chad actually enjoyed the story immensely but even before he could respond, Chad received yet another story in the mail.

This story was about a great athlete who started out playing hockey but who tired of his old sport, started swimming, and ended up in the Olympics. Luke wrote, "I wrote this because I knew that you could do all of this if you wanted to." Chad was alternately mesmerized and horrified as he read. All of the character failings that Chad thought were so well hidden, like his inability to stick to one endeavor for any considerable period of time, came to life in his brother's story. But it was impossible for Chad not to recognize that he had also been painted with deep affection and admiration by a young artist.

Chad could not wait to write a letter; he had to talk to his brother. "Your stories were incredible," Chad blurted, "unbelievably good. I think you have what it takes to become a really great writer. I'm beginning to wonder who the lucky brother really is."

The Friend

Alex came home from the hair salon, put on her best party dress, and inspected her makeup. Tonight she would be dining at the most exclusive and expensive restaurant at the lake resort where her parents rented a cabin. While it was her old friend Victor, who had always had a crush on Alex, who had invited her to the dinner, it was Victor's visiting cousin Carlos that she was really interested in. The three of them had played tennis that afternoon and Alex couldn't wait to see the handsome and sophisticated Carlos again.

Alex had persuaded her father that she could handle the family's small motorboat by herself for the brief trip to the restaurant dock. After all, she drove the boat more than anyone else in the family did! Alex drove very slowly so that her hairdo would still be perfect when she arrived. Soon she pulled up to the dock in her tiny boat amid all of the expensive yachts and powerboats, and she was glad to see that Victor and Carlos were waiting for her. Both young men were dressed in their finest clothes, but Alex had eyes only for Carlos.

Alex turned the motor off and let the boat slowly drift closer to the dock, eager to display her boating skills. But as she stretched out with the rope to tie up the boat, she nearly lost her balance. Fortunately, she was able to grab and hold on to the end of the pier. To her horror, Alex realized that the boat was drifting further away from the dock with her feet clinging desperately to its rail. Victor immediately jumped down to the lower dock to try to help, but he was too late. With a sickening splash, Alex fell headlong into the murky water next to the dock. Even though Alex was an excellent swimmer and certainly in no danger, swimming was the furthest thing from her mind. She was completely dismayed at the thought of having to face all of the people who had gathered at the dock watching her. They were all very polite and sympathetic; only Carlos could not hide his amusement. Victor tried to coax Alex toward his outstretched hand, but Alex preferred to stay in the water. With her dream evening completely ruined, Alex simply could not bear the thought of facing the rapidly growing crowd of people on the dock.

Suddenly Victor called, "Hold on, Alex! I'm coming to save you!" She watched in utter disbelief as Victor leaped into the water with a tremendous splash and surfaced next to her with a huge grin. Despite her distress, Alex couldn't help but smile and soon the two of them were hugging each other and laughing so hard that they couldn't stop. When Victor helped Alex from the water, somehow she didn't mind the crowd of now-smiling onlookers nearly as much as she thought she would. Victor whispered to her, "Let's go home and change and then we'll go out and get a pizza." During the boat ride back to her house, Alex watched her old friend laugh and shiver and joke about their experience, trying very successfully to cheer her up. Alex had to admit to herself that, despite the embarrassment, she had learned a great deal that night about true friends.

Exaggeration

This was Becky's first trip to the principal's office, and the knot in the pit of her stomach was sending notice that perhaps she had gone too far this time. It had all started so innocently, with Becky bragging to Claire about what a remarkable detective she was. She had convinced herself that the mysterious boy who sat alone in the back of their bus was the person who had been breaking into local pharmacies. "After all, he never talks to anyone! And I heard that the thief has a scar in the middle of his forehead. The other day his cap slid up and I swear that right in the middle of his forehead was the scar. I know that's him!" she told Claire emphatically. How could she have known that Claire would regard it as her civic duty to report the matter to her parents, who had promptly notified the police? If only Claire had asked first, Becky could have told her that even the best of detectives is never totally sure.

Now Becky was in serious trouble and it was all because of Claire and her stupid civic duty! How could she have known that Claire's father was related to the police captain? "She has always been one to make much ado about nothing," thought Becky, the knots still twisting in her stomach.

The situation quickly went from bad to worse when Becky spotted the school counselor walking down the hall into the principal's office. Becky was convinced that the counselor despised her and the thought of having her present during the meeting with the principal made her blood run cold. Everyone knew that counselors could positively demolish your chances to get into college. "That's why a counselor shouldn't be taking such innocent conversation so seriously," thought Becky. She remembered their last meeting and the counselor's stern lecture. "Your gossiping nearly ruined the reputation of a very innocent person," the counselor had told Becky. Becky remembered thinking that a counselor, of all people, should know that kids always talk about other kids. "Why single me out?" Becky thought.

Finally Becky was called into the office, and was immediately dismayed to find that the counselor had been placed in charge of the meeting. Once again she chided Becky for carelessly ruining an innocent person's reputation. But the worst part was the seriousness of having the police investigate a student for criminal activity. The principal sat and silently watched Becky and then finally took over the meeting. At first it was the softness in the principal's voice that captured Becky's attention. Then it was the story she told of the young man whom Becky had accused that really hit home. The principal told of his struggles with depression. She spoke of the concern of his parents that because of his embarrassment with the rumors about him, he had become reluctant to even attend school. Becky fought back the tears as she began to realize how much her loose tongue may have hurt another person. And then suddenly it all became clear to her. How could these people expect her to know everything about everyone's life? She knew nothing about the boy she had accused. If she had, that would have been a very different story. Becky knew better than to reveal her anger openly, but she folded her arms and seethed inside at the unfairness of it all.

The Rodeo

Rose sat by the window, unafraid despite the fact that she was flying to Montana alone for the first time. She had taken this flight with her family at least five times, but always their family vacation was over in two weeks. This time she would be spending the entire summer at her uncle's ranch and she could hardly contain her excitement. Rose couldn't wait to show the family how much her riding had improved, and in fact, she knew that she was finally good enough to compete in the rodeo held every year in late August.

She knew that her success in the rodeo would depend on the skills that she sharpened and her skills were now considerable. The hours of practice she had put in with handling a rope were bound to pay off. And although she had never practiced actually roping a steer, she was confident that the combination of her skill with a rope and her favorite horse, Streak, would make an unbeatable team. Rose closed her eyes and gleefully imagined her name being called as the top finisher in the calf roping competition. She especially savored the thought of beating her cousin Cindy.

Rose finally arrived at the ranch and when the interminable welcomes were finally over, she wasted no time running to the corral to see Streak. Rose was an expert in saddling and mounting a horse and she was convinced that before very long, she would be an expert in calf roping. But she was not prepared when Cindy suggested that riding Streak in the calf roping contest might not be a good idea. She offered to let Rose ride her own horse, Lightning. But Rose brushed off the thought, insisting that Streak was the horse she was most familiar with, and Cindy quickly changed the subject.

Rose immediately began to practice roping real calves but she had much more difficulty than she expected. She could throw the rope around a calf's neck but she could not seem to control the calf after that. Still she resisted Cindy's suggestion. She decided not to share her frustration with anyone. After nearly two weeks of nonstop failure, Rose resolved to study very carefully the technique used by Cindy and Lightning. Almost immediately, she realized that as soon as Cindy threw the rope, Lightning stopped and backed up. This backing up was what kept the rope tight. Suddenly the light bulb went off in Rose's mind. Until that very moment she had been convinced that her success depended solely on her own skills, but suddenly she realized that even this sport was a team effort.

With only three weeks until rodeo night, Rose knew that she would not have enough time to learn to ride Lightning. On the day of the rodeo, she watched her cousin Cindy rope a calf in the quickest time and win the trophy for the Girls' Calf Roping Contest. She fought back her feelings of jealousy and consoled herself with the thought that she would be ready next year.

As she flew back home, Rose thought about the chances she had missed this summer with sadness. She forced herself to remember how funny the rodeo clowns had been. Suddenly, she realized that the only time the clowns were used was during the bull riding competition. Any rider who fell would need the clown to attract the attention of the bull and keep him safe from the bull's sharp horns. "There it is again," Rose thought, "teamwork."

The Magician

Soon after the death of his father, the longstanding court magician to the Austrian king, Petruccio was named by the king to assume the post and to follow in his illustrious father's footsteps. As the magician, Petruccio would be one of the most important and trusted figures in the king's court, since the king would rely on him for advice ranging from the most trivial of decisions to essential matters of state. He would be expected to foretell future events by reading the stars and he was also supposed to ward off evil spirits who might bring harm to the kingdom.

Petruccio's father had loved his son dearly and sent him to the finest university in the world but his study of logic and science at the university left Petruccio ill-equipped to traffic in spirits and "read" the stars. He wanted nothing to do with the magic and superstition associated with the work that his father had done. How could he be expected to function as a court magician when he did not believe in what he was expected to do? Petruccio's worries and beliefs, however, mattered little to the court officials. The king needed a magician and there was no point in arguing with the king.

When he finally assumed the post of magician, Petruccio noticed danger and intrigue all around him. He was surrounded by men and women who were intensely jealous of the influence he had on the king. They would be watching Petruccio closely to see if there were some way that they could supplant him as the king's advisor and closest confidant. To make matters worse, it was clear that the king expected the right advice from his magician, and Petruccio had no idea how to provide that advice. But the young man was a swift learner and he quickly realized that the best way to survive life in the king's court was to make the fewest predictions possible. He also developed the skill of taking credit for whatever good befell the kingdom. When the king asked him to predict future events, Petruccio would make predictions for which he had the best chance of being correct. Once the king asked Petruccio to predict whether his soon-to-be-born child would be male or female. Petruccio noted that the king already had four sons and only one daughter and so he correctly predicted the birth of a son. But after several years of good fortune, Petruccio's luck ran out. When the king's favorite aunt fell ill with the fever, Petruccio was asked to predict her fate. He observed that more people who had contracted the disease had died than who had survived. Thus he predicted that the aunt would die.

Petruccio was unfortunately correct, but he had not anticipated that the king would blame him for the death of his beloved aunt. Nor would he have any way of knowing that the king had begun to suspect that his "magician" was a fraud. Having resolved to behead his unlucky court magician, the king called Petruccio before him. On his way to the king's chambers, Petruccio noticed an unusually large number of the king's guards in the halls and even spotted the king's executioner outside the door. With an ironic smile, the king asked him to foretell the manner in which he, Petruccio, would die. But the quick-thinking young man sensed the danger and he said to the king, "Your Majesty, I will die exactly four weeks before you." The king was dumbfounded. He had begun to suspect that his young magician was deceiving him, but how could he risk beheading him now? After all, Petruccio had been right in his predictions many times before. So instead of ordering his execution, the king ordered his guard to place Petruccio under special protection. He even commanded that they take care to be sure that all of Petruccio's needs and desires were met. And so Petruccio lived for many years in comfort and luxury under the watchful care of his king.

Mom's Lesson

Jane smiled when she remembered how foolish she had been to feel apprehensive about high school. She loved everything about it, and best of all, she had been singled out by the most popular girls in the school as a potential initiate in their group. One day Jane was walking through the halls with her fashionable friends, flaunting her newfound popularity, almost sensing the envy of the other girls, when she made her initial social blunder. Spotting her older brother Bruce in the hall heading toward the Special Education classroom, she broke into an enormous smile and waved eagerly to him. When Bruce returned her smile and waved back, one of Jane's companions inquired, "Who's the retarded guy?" Jane was baffled with her own response, as she reddened with embarrassment and heard herself respond in barely a whisper, "That's my brother."

Over the next few weeks, Jane had to face the most serious dilemma of her high school career. It was part of the family legend that Jane's parents would never consent, despite his Down syndrome, to an education that included lower expectations. They were convinced that Bruce could learn to read and write and Bruce, with his own internal sense of pride and with his work ethic, had surpassed even their wildest expectations. When he had turned sixteen and obtained a part-time job at a local pharmacy, an outsider might have thought that he had been elected president. But now Jane was having a troublesome time maintaining that sense of family pride. She even found, to her horror, that she was pretending to be preoccupied when Bruce waved or hurrying off under any pretext when he stopped to talk to her. Jane couldn't even muster the courage to share her problem with her parents.

And then the situation went from bad to worse with Bruce's dinner announcement that he had won a speaking part in the school's play. Jane could visualize the entire scenario, with Bruce, his name on the program, for all of her friends to gawk at. For Jane, high school had become no longer an exciting but a dreadful place, and the worst part of all was her guilt.

Finally Jane could stand it no longer and, gathering her resolve, spilled the details of her situation to her mother. She asked her to think of some reason that Bruce could not appear in the play, positive that she would understand, but disappointed that the only assurance that her mother would furnish was "Let me see what I can do."

The following week, Jane was annoyed at her mother's insistent invitation to have dinner with her old friend from high school. "I invited her just so that you could meet her," she retorted, when Jane protested about the impending evening of boredom. The evening turned out to be anything but boring.

Mother greeted her guest warmly and then sat in silence as her friend launched into a morbid monologue about being fired from several jobs, blaming everyone from her bosses to her fellow workers, when it was clear to Jane that her insensitivity was the primary cause of her own problems. Then she shifted to her string of three failed marriages, claiming that her life was so hectic that she regrettably had little time to spend with her children. The remainder of the evening consisted largely of more of the same.

When the evening was over, her mother confided to Jane, "You have no idea how hard I tried in school to make sure that girl became my friend. Sometimes I even ignored my own family. Trying to impress her, I hurt the people who stood by me throughout my entire life. I wish I knew then what I know now!"

That night it was guilt and remorse that led Jane to her mother. "Mom," said Jane, "you invited her so I could see and I really did. I wish I had never asked you to keep Bruce out of the play." "I've forgotten it already," she said with the biggest of smiles. "Sometimes our best learning comes from our greatest sorrows."

The Award Ceremony

Fred could never admit to anyone the mixed feelings that he experienced at the approach of the school's Sports Awards Banquet. His younger brother Mike was about to become the school's only freshman ever named as varsity football Player of the Year. Fred vividly remembered the moment when the head football coach shared with him, in confidence, that Mike would receive the award. With his arm around Fred, the coach whispered, "A lot of people will give me credit for bringing a freshman along so quickly, but I know that you've always been his true coach."

As Fred waited for the ceremony to start, he surmised that he would receive the Outstanding Bowler Award. Fred recalled his first encounters with competitive bowling. He was a freshman as well, about to take his own place on the varsity football team when he was diagnosed with scoliosis, a curvature of the spine. Fred's mother had noticed that his clothes were not fitting him properly and she began to worry. Fred brushed off her concerns but the family doctor did not. Then came the round of diagnostic tests and the report that, while he had a mild case, it could worsen if Fred continued playing the sport that he loved. Fred alternated between bouts of self-pity and feelings of resentment that his younger brother could still play. Fred felt guilty that his father wasn't comfortable sharing his enthusiasm about Mike's success, fearing an affront to Fred, but he still couldn't help himself. Finally, he accepted his father's advice and found a sport that was less risky than football. That was the beginning of his involvement with bowling.

Despite Fred's own disappointment, there was always something about his younger brother's spirit that fueled Fred's desire to mentor him. As he watched Mike play, he could envision himself ready to throw, locating the open receiver, and faking out his opponent. And Mike was the perfect student, always open to any suggestion, soaking up Fred's athletic know-how like a sponge. But it wasn't until Fred had confronted his medical condition and accepted bowling as his sport that he and his brother had become the perfect team. It had all really boiled down to two qualities: Fred's acceptance of his circumstances and his willingness to take a risk. Of course Fred knew that success in bowling would never even approximate the rewards of success in football. But at least now his father could be comfortable enough to openly enjoy his younger son's success.

The football coach was the first to be invited to the microphone and he began by reciting Mike's statistics, pointing out that his success had far surpassed that of any freshman in the history of the school. Then Fred groaned inwardly when Mike was called upon to make an acceptance speech. If they did the same thing for everyone, the banquet would go on all night.

When Mike appeared on stage, he began by saying, "I am really only half-owner of this award," looking directly at Fred as he spoke. "It was my body that was running plays, but it was my brother that my brain was listening to and I never would have had that knowledge without Fred. I asked Coach if his name could be added to this award. I'd like to introduce you to the other Player of the Year, my big brother Fred." As he finished speaking, Mike motioned for Fred to join him at the podium.

Fred was truly dumbfounded by what had just happened but as he stood with his brother's arm around him and looked out at the cheering crowd, he saw something that stunned him even more. He had never once seen his father cry but there he stood, unashamed, with tears streaming down his cheeks. Fred could see his father's pride written all over him and Fred was simply grateful that he had the good fortune or the good sense just for once to put someone else first in his life.

Tutor of the Year

Chet was startled to see Lori biking up his driveway calling, "Get your bike, lazy one, cause you're not the only one who needs exercise." Chet wondered where in the world she had found such a ramshackle secondhand bike. Just a few weeks ago she had given her new bike to a neighborhood family who had come on hard times. Lori was Chet's best friend, and he sometimes recalled with relief the fact that in elementary school he had been confident enough to ignore the teasing of his friends about his supposed "girlfriend." Now his friends agreed, even if sometimes grudgingly, that her wit and contagious laugh simply made her easy to be with.

"I thought that you would be practicing your roller blading today," Chet said as they started down the bike path. "No, I needed a change and besides I thought I'd put my energies into mountain biking," replied Lori. Lori told herself that the fact that Chet could not skate but was an avid biker had nothing to do with the matter, but in reality, she had already decided that biking would be more fun than blading if she could spend that time with Chet.

In fact, when Chet made the varsity basketball team last semester, Lori was left with a great deal of time on her hands. She had always excelled in mathematics and so she volunteered to work with younger students who were having difficulty in geometry and trigonometry. Chet still remembered that excited phone call, with Lori talking nonstop about how much she had helped the student she worked with, the one whom everyone else regarded as a troublemaker. He couldn't help but remember the day the following year when Lori was honored as the school's Tutor of the Year.

Several days after their afternoon bike ride, Chet appeared in Lori's driveway carrying a pair of secondhand roller blades in an old case. "Turnaround is fair play," he called and then he shouted, "Grab your blades and let's go!" Lori, her mouth wide open, finally blurted out, "You don't even know how to ice skate." "Yes, but don't forget, my friend is the tutor of the year and she'll be able to teach me everything I need to know."

Lori knew that Chet had excelled at any sport he had ever tried, so she was not surprised at his confidence as he strapped on his skates and stood in the deserted parking lot where Lori practiced. But when Chet asked "What do I do now?" Lori looked stunned and replied, "You just kind of move your feet." "Can't you do a little better than that?" he asked, obviously surprised that Lori could not describe the mechanics of skating. An obviously embarrassed Lori quickly scanned the parking lot and finally suggested, "Why don't you just face downhill over there and I'm sure that will get you moving." Lori was right, but she couldn't explain to Chet how to stop either, so Chet spent a good deal of time that afternoon hugging the pavement. Needless to say, he spent even more time teasing Lori about her lack of teaching techniques.

Despite the rocky start, Chet was determined to master roller blading but, as luck would have it, Lori cut her ankle badly on a sharp rock while mountain biking with Chet. She had to avoid the strain of the roller blade boot for three weeks. And while Chet visited his friend often, he also was determined that he would spend at least an hour each day practicing his roller blading. When Lori's foot had finally healed, Chet coaxed her into an afternoon of roller blading under the pretext that he needed more instruction and practice. He relished the moment as he literally skated circles around his former tutor, having far surpassed her in skill and speed in just three weeks. Lori stood with her jaw wide open, and then grinned at her friend, partly in admiration, partly in envy, and, she had to admit, partly in annoyance as well.

The Hero

Even though nearly three years had passed, Chuck could still feel the pain of his father's disappointment. How could he forget the years that his parents scrimped and worked to send Chuck to the best private school on the island, convinced that a good education would get him into law school in the States? Chuck's father wanted him to become a lawyer, not for the money, but for the chance to return to the island and work to improve the lives of the islanders. When Chuck had dropped out of law school and accepted a position as deputy for freight operations at the island's port facility, his father was devastated and the strain in their relationship had lasted until this very day.

But as painful as these thoughts still were, Chuck almost welcomed them on this day, for they at least took his mind off his most immediate and pressing problem: what to do about Dan. Chuck was the captain of the small but powerful tugboat that guided all military, freight, and vacation cruises into the island. For several weeks he had observed his old school friend, locked in frequent animated conversation at a dockside bar with a particularly unsavory freight hauler, and Chuck couldn't help but become suspicious.

Once his curiosity had been piqued Chuck decided to investigate further, and how he regretted that decision. It was never so much the fact that his investigation brought him into danger for his life, but it was the fact that Dan seemed to be involved up to his ears in a local drug smuggling and distribution ring. Now, as he waited for Ed to arrive at the restaurant for their weekly breakfast, Chuck was both brokenhearted and terribly torn. After all, Chuck couldn't forget that he, Ed, and Dan had been inseparable friends throughout their youth, at least until Chuck had begun to attend his private school.

Finally Ed arrived, resplendent in his dress uniform and armed with his familiar smile. Even though Ed had received the Coast Guard appointment that Chuck had coveted, he could never bring himself to resent his old friend. Ed's smile soon disappeared as Chuck outlined the evidence that he had gathered, and when he had finished, Chuck was deeply surprised that Ed did not hesitate for even an instant. Ed intended to immediately turn in all the evidence to the local authorities. Of course, Chuck knew that the evidence could not be suppressed, and although he was relieved that it would not have to be him that did it, he was also surprised that Ed seemed to have no misgivings about turning in Dan. He had some inkling of the situation when he heard Ed whisper to himself, "Wait till you see what this does for my career!"

In the weeks that followed, Ed became a local hero, his picture plastered all over the island's newspaper. Each time it was Ed who was credited with the removal of millions of dollars of drugs from the local streets of the island. And even though no one seemed to realize that it was Chuck who had unearthed the only significant evidence in the case, Chuck couldn't bring himself to resent that fact. After all, no one could know that he was the one who had turned in an old friend.

The following week, Chuck answered the knock on his apartment door and was stunned to see his father standing in the hall. "If you have the time, I'd like us to have lunch together at our old restaurant," he said. "For you, Dad, I always have the time," Chuck responded with a broad smile. At the restaurant, his father told how he had learned of Chuck's role in breaking up the smuggling ring. "I always wanted you to help the people of this island to have a better life," said Chuck's father, "but I realize that I wanted that to happen on my terms, and not yours. I'm both proud of you and sorry for the way that I've behaved." "Forget it, Dad. It's just great to have you back again."

The Duck Hunter

When Grandfather had haltingly confided from his hospital bed that he had been selected by the National Duck Hunting Association for its Lifetime Service Award, Bill had nearly burst with pride, but his enthusiasm quickly waned when Grandfather asked Bill to accept the award in his stead. Bill would have to deliver an acceptance speech! "He knows that my stuttering gets heavy whenever I get nervous, so how could he ask me to make a speech for him?"

"It's such a shame that he had that stroke because getting that award and giving that speech would have been one of the highlights of his life," Bill's mother sighed on their drive home. "If he weren't so self-conscious about how the stroke affected his speech, he could go to the banquet himself." "But where does that leave me?" moaned Bill. "Why don't you talk to Mr. Brock about it?" suggested mother, knowing that Bill admired his former speech therapist and that he always seemed to have good advice for Bill.

Mr. Brock first listened patiently to Bill's worries and self-doubts, and then suggested an intriguing idea. To alleviate his nervousness, Bill could imagine his acceptance speech as a conversation with his grandfather. That way, he could try to block out the audience completely and imagine that he and Grandfather were the only people in the room. Mr. Brock warned Bill that such a technique would take much practice and discipline, but he was confident that Bill could master it.

And so Bill began to prepare for his speech, reflecting on the events in his life with Grandfather that stood out most saliently in his mind. Bill practiced his speech diligently for weeks but when the moment finally arrived, he approached the podium with more dread than confidence. But as Mr. Brock had suggested, Bill firmly focused his attention on a mental picture of his grandfather. He knew that his opening remarks would be the most difficult part of his speech: "My grandfather asked me to accept this award and to take his place at this banquet, but I know that that is impossible. And I know how well you all know him and how much he has loved and contributed to this organization. But what you may not know is what my grandfather has meant in the lives of so many people. So I would like to speak to my grandfather from my heart, just as if he were right here with us."

Bill turned slightly toward the empty chair he had placed near the podium and began to speak. He reminded Grandfather of the time when Bill was six and he had been allowed to watch Grandfather train Molly, his new Labrador retriever. "You told me I had to sit quietly and watch while you threw decoys into the bay and began teaching the proper commands to Molly. And when I couldn't just sit any longer and I called to Molly so that I could hug her, I wasn't really prepared for how stern your lecture was. That was only my first experience with your appreciation for discipline and obedience as the keys to success, but it certainly wasn't my last."

Bill went on to tell his grandfather how grateful he was that he modeled the importance of facing personal challenges, and most of all, for the way in which Grandfather helped Bill face his biggest challenge, stuttering. "It was you who noticed my embarrassment and withdrawal, you who arranged for me to meet with an expert language pathologist, you who helped me understand that stuttering is not an emotional problem. You showed me that there was nothing wrong with me as a person, that it was tension in the speech muscles that caused stuttering, and that hard work and discipline could help me overcome it."

"I always knew you had faith in my ability to face challenges and now I understand why you asked me to be here tonight. I think you knew that this speech would be one of the biggest challenges of my life, but I also know that it was you who gave me the tools I needed to succeed. This audience thanks you for your service to this organization, but I thank you for all that you've meant to my life."

The Injury

It seemed that the entire town was trying to fit into the Franklin High School football stadium for the final game of the season. But the buzz in the crowd was all about the recruiters from big-name colleges who had come to scout Ron, their local football and baseball hero. It seemed that their small town was finally on the map and it was a fine athlete and a fine young man who had put them there. At the end of the evening few people at the game even remembered the final score. The images that seem engraved on the minds of everyone at the game were the hard tackle, the awkward fall and the stretcher that carried Ron to the ambulance that waited outside the field for just such emergencies. The diagnosis was grim. A torn rotator cuff would need immediate surgical repair and months of rehabilitation and there were no guarantees that Ron would ever regain the athletic skills that had set him apart from every other player in the entire league.

On his way to the hospital, Ron thought about his father who would be anxiously praying and waiting for him there. Ron knew that his father had taken on the extra part time job to earn the money to cover the expenses for Ron's participation in sports. His father had always been proud of his son's athletic success but Ron suspected that he was most grateful for the full scholarship it would bring, a scholarship to a private university that the family could never have afforded.

With that scholarship now in jeopardy, Ron knew that he would have to face some thorny decisions with some far-reaching consequences. But unfortunate decisions and still more regrettable consequences were things that Ron and his father had talked about for as long as Ron could remember. His father had dropped out of football because he hadn't kept up his grades and then he had to watch his best friend, a player whom everyone recognized was not his father's equal, go on to win a football scholarship to a top-grade university and to have a thoroughly successful college career. How many times had he heard his father speculate wistfully on what might have been if he had only stayed with football. After graduation and a tour of duty in Vietnam, his father had returned determined to go on to earn a college degree, but after several months in the local community college, he became jealous of the spending money that his working friends always seemed to have. He dropped out of college and took a full-time job, but he still somehow never seemed to earn enough or succeed enough to match his aspirations. Whenever he could,

Ron's father would make a point of identifying the consequences he had paid and still continued to pay because of the poor decisions he had made in his youth and Ron knew that his father would be deeply disappointed in him if he made the wrong decision.

After his surgery, Ron's physical therapy was more painful than anything he had ever experienced. He began to wonder whether he really wanted to risk reinjuring the shoulder by trying to rejoin the team, but without football, what could he do to afford college? He had always been an honor roll student, but he knew that he would never qualify for an academic scholarship. Ron began to wonder whether he should drop out of sports altogether. Then he would have more time to devote to his studies. But what about the regrets that were sure to come later? What about the consequences if he made the wrong decision?

His father accompanied Ron, as always, to the doctor's office at the end of Ron's physical therapy program. The doctor told them what Ron had suspected all along: He could return to football but another injury to the shoulder could leave him with permanent damage and pain. Ron and his father drove in silence to the coffee shop where they had spent countless hours over the years discussing life's choices and consequences.

Ron wanted desperately to ask his father what he should do, but he sensed that the time for letting others decide for him had long since passed. Instead, Ron turned to his father and said, "You've never told me which regret was greater, dropping out of football or out of college."

To Ron's surprise, his father replied, "I'm really beginning to wonder if I've wasted too much of my life regretting the things that I've done. If I had stayed in college and in football, I may never have been fortunate enough to meet your mother or to have had a son like you. I may never have been nearly as contented as I've been over the years. I'm beginning to think that maybe it isn't always the choices that you make but what you make of the choices that really matters." Ron nodded; he didn't quite understand yet what his father meant but he had the distinct feeling that he soon would.

The Babysitter

Nancy spent her study hall period frantically working to finish her assignments so that she wouldn't be late for her meeting with her next-door neighbor, Jean. Today was the day that they would be finalizing plans for the birthday party of the great love in Nancy's life, Jean's adorable six year old son, Jeff. And now Nancy sat in Jean's kitchen and assisted Jean in making the arrangements to hire a clown, several ponies, and a tent, since for such a momentous occasion no expense could be spared. As they planned, Nancy and Jean laughed and reminisced about the day nearly six years ago when Nancy, quietly and cautiously standing behind her mother, came to meet their new neighbors with a plate of freshly baked cookies. Nancy was captivated by their tiny child and when Jean asked her if she would like to hold little Jeff, Nancy was thrilled to the soles of her feet. Nancy spent an entire hour cuddling the baby and right then and there a love for the little boy crawled its way into Nancy's heart, a love that was even stronger six years later.

And as an added bonus, Jean had become one of Nancy's closest friends and confidantes. Even when her own beloved mother occasionally lost her patience with Nancy, it seemed that Jean was always there with words of encouragement and advice, and Nancy treasured her friendship, even though Jean was fifteen years her senior. Nancy's reverie was interrupted by a demanding voice from upstairs. "Hey Nan, I can't get my computer game to work." Nancy promptly stopped filling out invitations and immediately ran upstairs to help Jeff and when she returned, she found Jean shaking her head in mock exasperation. "Did you ever notice that Jeff wouldn't even try to do that to anyone else? Sometimes I feel like scolding him when he takes advantage of you and just assumes you'll drop everything for him." Nancy grinned, confident that both Jean and Jeff loved her and that spoiling Jeff occasionally would do no real harm. But strangely enough, Jean's words made her recall how she had always been puzzled and somewhat resentful that her friends closer to her own age didn't seem to share her affection for Jeff.

The following Saturday, Nancy picked up Jeff at midmorning and Jean reminded him to follow all the rules: "You stay close to Nancy and listen to everything she tells you." Jeff and Nancy smiled patiently at Jean's lecture, both fully aware that between them, there were precious few rules to speak of. Then they departed for the theater for the first part of Jeff's birthday present, a movie that Jeff had been impatient to see. When the feature had concluded and she and Jeff were exiting the theater, Nancy noticed a large travel poster of London, pointed to it and excitedly told Jeff, "That's the place where I'm going this summer!" Nancy spoke breathlessly of her acceptance into a summer program at Oxford and about the kinds of sights she expected to see in London, but when she turned to look at Jeff, he was nowhere to be found.

Nancy's search for her lost charge became more frantic by the moment as she pushed her way past people, calling Jeff's name. With every passing moment she envisioned having to confess to Jean that her son was lost, maybe kidnapped, maybe even worse, and that it was all her fault! Now in tears of panic, Nancy rushed to the theater concession stand and begged hysterically for someone to help her find a missing child. The rush of concerned workers, each of them asking different questions about who the boy was and what he looked like, nearly overwhelmed Nancy.

She was on the verge of completely losing control when she spied Jeff, nonchalantly walking out of the theater's game room. For the first time ever, Nancy scolded Jeff for his lack of consideration, and Jeff responded, "Aw, women make such a big deal out of everything." Behind clenched teeth, Nancy muttered some words of thanks to her would-be helpers, grabbed Jeff's hand, and led him firmly back to the car. "Hey, what about the train ride you promised me?" he cried. "You lost that when you broke the rules!" she retorted. Jeff cried all the way home and there was a time that she would have done anything to dry one of Jeff's tears, but this time Nancy found herself curiously unmoved and she had the distinct feeling that her days of spoiling Jeff were over.

Dreams and Vision

"Don't touch those slides! I haven't studied them yet!" snapped Len, with enough volume and vehemence to startle his longtime lab partner. When Len realized what he had done and sensed his partner's discomfort, he quickly apologized, muttering something about having a miserable day. Bert knew his old friend well enough to distinguish between a bad day and some deep trouble, but Bert also knew that Len was not about to admit that anything was bothering him. The private boarding school that they both attended on scholarships was a long way from home. But Mr. Lunder, their advanced placement science teacher, had become Len's father in absentia. And though he knew Len would not appreciate the intrusion, Bert made it a point to see if Mr. Lunder had noticed a change in his prize pupil and, if he had, to see if he had discovered its source.

As it seems, Mr. Lunder had indeed noticed a great deal of edginess and anxiety creep into the normally pleasant personality of Len, and he was determined to find out what was wrong. Unfortunately, he also knew that coaxing information out of Len was akin to pulling teeth. With little to lose, Mr. Lunder decided to try the direct approach and ask Len if something was bothering him. He was stunned to listen to Len, without any provocation at all, disclose the fact that his vision had become increasingly blurred over the past several weeks and that Len had become convinced that he was losing his sight altogether.

Later that afternoon, Mr. Lunder left the principal's office with Len in tow, having made all the necessary legal arrangements to take Len to the eye doctor's office. Mr. Lunder tried to distract his melancholy young charge from his gloomy and fatalistic ideas of life and health. He chatted about the advantages Len and his classmates would have as freshmen in college with all of the advanced placement courses they had completed in mathematics and science. Throughout the ride Len nodded dully or responded in monosyllables, his mind millions of miles away in the realm of dejection and despair. Fortunately, it was a completely different Len on the ride home, for the ophthalmologist had diagnosed an eye infection as the cause of the blurred vision, a problem that could be cleared up in less than a week with simple eye drops.

Mr. Lunder fought off the temptation to say "I told you so" to his young charge, and resolved to keep an eye on Len and watch his spirits rise as his vision improved, but unfortunately, the smile did not return. Instead Len appeared at his door two days later and announced that he was dropping out of school and returning home. "It's all over, Mr. Lunder," said Len, fighting back his tears. "My eyes are getting worse and I think I'm in real trouble. All those dreams of going to medical school and getting my mom and sister into a nice neighborhood are all over, and to make matters worse, I'm going to go blind and be a burden on my whole family." This time Mr. Lunder did not bother dissuading Len, but merely obtained authorization to take Len to the famous eye hospital in the city near their school.

Len had a sense of awe just walking into the eye hospital where researchers and physicians conducted the kind of research he had dreamed of doing. He also felt a confidence that he had not felt before, one that was well rewarded. It seems that there had been no eye infection after all, but that the problem lay in the type of contact lens that Len had been wearing for years. His eye had become extremely irritated but would improve rapidly once he began to use the temporary glasses and rid himself of his current supply of contact lenses. "After several months' rest from my contacts, they are going to give me some temporary ones that they will monitor to be sure that I am wearing the right kind," he reported gleefully. Mr. Lunder felt as if a mountain had just rolled off his back as he told Len, "It looks as if your dreams are back on, Len, but one of these days, you and I are going to have to have a long talk."

Differences

Lin sat thinking in silence in the rear seat of the car as her parents drove out of the tree-lined main drive of the idyllic university campus and began the long ride home. But there was no reflection of the campus serenity in Lin's mind that morning. She was trying desperately to control her anger as she relived the events of the past few days, events that dragged her memories back to the days of her youth when she felt so much like an outsider. The cinema in her mind replayed the first time that Lin had met her best friends, Marilyn and Cindy. Lin was seven years old and her family had just moved into their new home when her mother called her to tell her that two girls had knocked at the front door and asked if they could play with Lin.

The three girls sat on the front porch as her new friends bombarded Lin with questions about her life in China. She had all but forgotten the queasy feeling that came over her, like being a strange specimen captured in a bottle to be scrutinized by inquisitive students. "They don't want to be my friends," Lin blurted out to her mother late one afternoon, "they just want to show me how different I am and I don't want to play with them again." But Lin's mother simply said, "Are you talking about how they feel or how you feel?" And so Lin decided not to run away and soon she joined Marilyn and Cindy in their imaginary world in the nearby woods, reading stories of faraway lands. Within months, the girls had become inseparable and they were still the best of friends at the end of their junior year at the university. But it was the memory of being seven years old and feeling so terribly and unalterably different that consumed Lin during the ride home, and not the friendship or the happy ending.

"You're pretty quiet, Lin," Mother said, but Lin was slow to respond, for it had been her mother's idea for Lin to become acquainted with the four Chinese exchange students who began their university studies that semester. At that time Lin thought that serving as their mentor and assisting them in making the transition to American life and customs would be a marvelous way to help the girls, but their initial meeting had not been as fruitful as Lin had hoped it would be. At first, the girls sat in rapt attention and laughed as Lin shared with them stories of how she and her friends had learned to navigate the sometimes rough waters of the often convoluted campus procedures and protocol. But when Lin began to ask about their customs and point out sharp contrasts between Chinese and American ideas of propriety and manners, the girls lapsed into an uncomfortable silence and soon were chattering nervously among themselves about Chinese poets and literature, books that Lin could not even read. The meeting ended awkwardly, with everyone sensing the presence of bruised egos but no one quite sure of their source.

"They seemed to relish making me feel like an outsider and you know, Mother, I can't really comprehend how a working knowledge of Chinese poetry will help them get very far in America."

Her mother replied, "Are you certain that is what they wanted you to feel, Lin? Perhaps it was awkward for them to seem so different from you and all of the other students."

"That's no excuse for being impolite," snapped Lin, "especially when I was going out of my way to try to help them."

Later that week, on the family's long-planned trip to Niagara Falls, Lin stood mesmerized by the swiftness and intensity of the river, all very familiar but yet always somehow new. She felt her mother slip her arm around her and heard her whisper, "The river always knows where it is going, perhaps because it knows where it has been." Lin knew her mother too well to believe that this was mere idle chatter; she had learned long ago that it was worth the effort to think long and hard to uncover the sometimes arcane lesson embedded in her mother's words.

Lin woke the next morning filled with a fresh resolve to help her new friends organize a discussion group to explore Chinese literature and culture, and she knew exactly whom she could invite to participate. The group would dedicate itself to the celebration of diversity, differences, and friendship in the university community, for as her mother knew well, it always helps to know where you've been.

The Psychology Class

Marty sauntered into his Child Psychology class and was elated to see the audiovisual equipment already set up and ready to run. Even as a university sophomore, Marty still loved to watch movies during class time. Child Psychology was his favorite class of all, but it always seemed to him that watching a video was much more enjoyable than reading dull books. After a short introduction, the psychology professor began the DVD. The class settled back to observe the exploits of a six year old boy named Mike who was so successful in getting his own way and dominating his parents that he had become the stuff of legends in Child Psychology.

The class watched with increasing amusement as Mike cajoled, whined, whimpered, and cried and essentially did whatever was necessary to impose his will on his parents. His hapless father seemed almost completely overmatched and utterly unable to handle his son. Despite his tough talk to the contrary, he caved in at the slightest hint of Mike's displeasure and gave the boy whatever he desired. The film showed Mike's father undergoing extensive indoctrination in appropriate child rearing practices, even arriving at the point where he could verbalize exactly what he was doing and why it was wrong. The mild amusement of the class gave way to loud bursts of laughter as Mike and his father promptly reverted to their original behavior patterns the moment the cameras began to roll again. There had been no learning taking place after all.

When the lights came up, the professor acknowledged the appreciative laughter of the class but quickly emphasized that such child rearing practices are no laughing matter for children like Mike. He went on to cite considerable research suggesting that such children often grow up lacking in self-discipline and resolve, with a powerful tendency to attribute their own shortcomings to others. Even worse, many grow into scheming and manipulative adults who use similar though more sophisticated tactics to get their own way in their adult relationships.

When the class had ended, Marty left distraught and ashen because the relationship he had seen depicted on film was so eerily similar to the relationship he had, not only with his father but also with his mother. Marty recalled an endless string of unpleasant episodes he had caused, all for the sake of an ice cream cone or a toy that they were reluctant to immediately procure for him. And he recalled with horror the conversation he had with his father not two days earlier, when he had wheedled some extra spending money by playing on his father's sympathies. Could it be that Marty too was doomed to become a lazy, scheming, manipulative adult whom no one could possibly stomach?

Marty frantically searched his memories of his relationship with his girlfriend, with his old and new classmates, even with his professors. Every instance of concessions that they had made, or arguments that he had won immediately became proof positive in Marty's mind that he was doomed to a life of failure and unhappiness, all because of his own selfishness as a child. When he could stand it no longer, Marty made an appointment to see his psychology professor, convinced that he needed professional help.

The professor listened patiently and quietly as Marty poured out his tale of woe. Then, leaning back in his chair, he said, "First of all, Marty, truly manipulative people have no idea that they are being manipulative. The very fact that you are aware of the possibility is a good sign that you are on the right track. There will always be times when you get your way and the same is true with others, and as long as the score is roughly even, you can be reasonably sure that you are OK. And as far as your parents are concerned, there comes a time in every child's life when he must decide what kind of relationship he will have with his father and mother, no matter what has gone on before. Maybe this is your time."

Marty left the professor's office unburdened by the great weight of guilt that he had piled upon himself, but also filled with a new resolve. Before the end of the day, he had accepted the part-time job that he had flatly refused to consider a few short weeks ago, determined that never again would he solicit his parents for money so that he could evade work. Payday produced a curiously proud moment for Marty when he mailed a generous check to his father, requesting that his parents have dinner at a restaurant together at his expense. "I hope I haven't been too big of a pain in the neck all these years," read the card, "but someday I'm going to make you proud of me."

The Retirement Community

Mr. Lancaster strolled the newly paved streets of the Daytona Retirement Community as he had done almost daily for the six months since he and his wife had relocated into their new villa. This was truly Lancaster's fantasy: a new community, a balmy climate (no more Michigan winters for him!), and best of all, no noisy children allowed. Lancaster passed dozens of manicured lawns and professionally landscaped gardens on his regular route through the almost eerie early morning tranquility of the neighborhood. Lancaster was proud that his exercise regimen and limited diet had him in the best physical condition he had seen in decades. And while community maintenance fees were rather steep, he would never have to mow a lawn again or worry if the roof leaked or if the garbage disposal jammed. All it took now was an expeditious phone call and any difficulty with the house or the grounds was immediately resolved.

Even Evelyn seemed to treasure their new life and her new circle of friends, despite her initial stubborn resistance to the move during those difficult days when she begged Lancaster to stay in the old house in Michigan, close to the children and grandchildren. Lancaster chuckled as he thought of his wife's hectic social calendar with the ladies' bridge club, her charity work at the church, her volunteer work at the local elementary school, and the seemingly endless round of planning committee meetings that her benevolent work entailed. True, Lancaster had his beloved golf, but even golfing three or four times a week did not seem to lift Lancaster's game to the level he had anticipated. And although he would never dare admit it to the rest of his regular foursome, he had begun to think that having the leisure to play endless rounds of golf was not all that it was cracked up to be. He had even briefly entertained the idea of seriously pursuing senior tennis, but his old knee injury sounded the alarm and quickly reminded him that he was no longer a spry youngster.

Lancaster stopped himself short; he had caught himself dwelling on the negative instead of the positive yet again. Lancaster had begun to think that his occasional descent into pessimism was something of a character flaw. What more could he possibly desire from his life? His lifestyle was the envy of nearly all of his old friends in Michigan, and Lancaster could not understand why he was beset by those exasperating, gnawing doubts. He knew that Evelyn missed seeing the grandchildren every day, but with phone calls and e-mails and electronically transmitted photographs, they could keep in touch with their children's and their grandchildren's lives almost daily, as Evelyn seldom failed to do. And Lancaster himself could never complain that he was bored, could he? So why did the conviction that he had made a terrible mistake keep cropping up with an increased and disturbing regularity? He had to keep one simple idea very clear in his mind: moving to Florida was not a mistake. He and Evelyn had worked diligently all of their lives to achieve this lifestyle and Lancaster was simply not going to tolerate this weakness. After all, in his professional career, he had drilled into countless protégés the importance of a disciplined mind and now it was time that he started to practice what he had preached.

Lancaster found it monumentally annoying that none of his circle of friends seemed to have any of the kinds of misgivings that haunted him. Only old Wenger would sometimes chide Lancaster with some old nonsense about getting a life and making himself useful, and Wenger would hardly qualify as one of Lancaster's inner circle. Wenger acted as if a forty year career in which Lancaster had risen through the ranks to become chief executive officer of a Fortune 500 company meant nothing! Lancaster knew that he had paid his dues and now it was time to reap the rewards.

Only one element of this entire state of affairs was certain: He could never share with Evelyn the misgivings that had cropped up so often in the past few months. He knew his wife far too well to think that she could easily weather the storm of doubts that would come from second-guessing the decision that had changed their lives so much for the better. One word about his doubts and he would be in for endless soul-searching sessions far into the early hours of morning after morning until they had finally resolved their "problem." No, Lancaster knew that he would have to keep his thoughts to himself.

Informational Passages

All Kinds of Trucks

A big, red fire truck goes fast.

It helps put out fires.

A small, green truck goes down the street.

It brings boxes to our store.

A tanker truck has a long, long hose.

It brings gas to our gas station.

A large blue truck sprays water.
It cleans our street.

The best truck rings its bell and plays a song.
It brings me a treat.

Plants

A man needs food.
He goes to the store.
He buys his food.

A cow needs food.
She walks to the grass.
She eats the grass.

A plant needs food.
It can not move.
It has to make its food.

The roots get the water.
The water moves to the leaf.
The leaf makes food.
The plant eats the food.

People eat the plants.
The plants are good for them.

See the Birds

See the birds.
The birds are in the sky.
The birds fly high.
Some birds are red.
Some birds are yellow.
You can not see the color.

See the birds.

The birds come to eat seeds.

Some birds are red.

Some birds are yellow.

You can see the color.

Do not go by the birds.

The birds will fly.

They may fly into a tree far away.

You will not see the color.

Turtles

Turtles can be big or small.

All turtles can crawl.

Some turtles can swim.

All turtles have shells.

A turtle can hide in its shell and be safe.

Small turtles make good pets.

They can live near a pond or a lake.

They eat worms, bugs, and grass.

Children often catch small turtles and take them home.

They can keep them in a large cage and take care of them.

They give the turtles water and food.

Large turtles live near the sea.

They catch their food in the sea.

They stay under the water for a long time.

They can swim very fast and can live a long time.

Planes and Trucks

A pilot can fly an airplane.
He takes people with him.
He takes goods with him.
He can go a long way but it does not take a long time.
People pay lots of money.

A lady can drive a truck.
She does not take people with her.
She takes goods with her.
She goes a long way too, but it will take a long time.
She carries things people need.

Some people do not like to fly.
They are afraid because the plane flies high and fast.
These people can drive in a car.
They will feel safe.
But they may not be so safe.
There are many cars and trucks on the roads.
There are not many planes in the sky.

Baby Lions

Baby lions are called cubs.
Baby lions are furry.
The cubs like to stay with the mother.

Baby lions like to play.
They run.
They jump.
They roll.

Baby lions like to eat.
They eat meat.
They eat grass.
They drink milk.
They drink water.

Baby lions like to sleep.
They sleep in the day.
It is too hot to play.
They like to nap under a tree.
A big lion keeps them safe.
Baby lions like to be clean.

They clean each other.
The mother licks them clean.

Baby lions like to play.
Baby lions like to eat.
Baby lions like to sleep.
Baby lions like to be clean.

Black Bears

Black bears live in the U.S.

They live near woods or near mountains.

They live in dens.

The dens can be inside a tree or a cave.

Bears sleep all winter.

In spring, they wake up hungry.

Sometimes they can't find enough food.

They like to eat berries, honey, nuts, and acorns.

But they will eat almost anything.

If they don't find food close to home, they go out looking.

One bear and her cubs could not find enough to eat.

They came down the mountain.

They broke into someone's house.

This was very dangerous.

They took cookies, dog food, and honey.

The cubs took burgers off the grill.

People found the cubs.

The cubs only weighed 20 pounds.

They should have weighed 50 pounds.

No wonder they were hungry.

People in Groups

Long ago people lived in groups.

They were called tribes.

They hunted and fished together.

They found plants and berries.

They moved on foot from place to place.

They followed the animals.

They only killed the animals they needed.

They did not grow their own food.

They had to work together to live.

Today people live in groups, too.

They live in cities and towns.

They still like to hunt and fish.

But now they grow their own food on farms.

They also raise their own animals.

But most people buy their food.

They have cars and planes to help them move.

But they still have to work together to live.

A Bird That Doesn't Fly

There is a bird that doesn't fly.

This bird loves to swim.

This bird lives in the cold.

This bird is a penguin.

Some penguins live at the South Pole.

They like to play and swim.

In the fall, they walk far.

They walk far to lay their egg.

The father penguin keeps the egg safe.

The mother penguin knows the baby will need food.

So, the mother penguin walks far to get food.

When she gets back, the egg is already hatched.

A baby penguin is born.

The father penguin is hungry.

The baby penguin wants food.

Only the mother penguin feeds the baby.

The father penguin has to walk far to get food for himself.

The mother and the baby and the father penguin will all get to eat.

Army Ants

Do you ever run from ants? Some people in South America do. They run from the army ants. The ants are only about the size of your fingernail. But they have large and strong jaws. Army ants march in very large numbers looking for food. They march very slowly in a row four feet wide. But most armies are more than a mile long. All animals must get out of their way. They can bite and kill large animals and they can even kill people.

Army ants are hard to stop. They can climb over walls and trees. Not even water can stop them. They just hold onto each other with their jaws and then roll themselves into a ball. Then they can float across rivers and streams! Sometimes the ants march close to a village. Then the people must all move out. But some of the people are glad to see the ants. The ants clean up the town for them by killing small animals and pests.

The Doctor Fish

Some animals are a big help to other animals. One animal that helps others is the wrasse. The wrasse is a fish about four inches long. He is very brightly colored. He lives in the South Pacific Ocean. He is like a doctor to other fish.

His office is in the rocks called reefs. Many fish come to the doctor for help. These fish have animals that live on their bodies. They would like to have them taken off. The wrasse eats these tiny animals. He also uses his teeth to clean wounds. He helps the fish to get better.

The doctor can be very busy. Sometimes he works all day. But the doctor gets his pay too! The doctor gets the food he likes from his patients. They also protect the doctor from bigger fish. But the doctor and his patients must be careful. A fish called the blenny looks just like the wrasse. Some fish think they are coming to see the doctor. Then the blenny takes a bite out of them! That makes things worse.

A Rose and a Sweet Pea

I have some rose bushes in my yard. They make a border for my flower garden. Their sharp thorns keep animals and pests away. Some of my rose plants are climbers. I put stakes by the plants so they can climb high.

Roses bloom all summer long. Even if I pick some flowers, more will bloom and they will not stop until winter comes. When it gets cold, the cell walls of the rose plant grow thick. This protects them from the cold and they will bloom again the next year.

I have many flowers called "sweet peas" in my garden. They come in many colors, they smell very nice, and they bloom all summer too. Most sweet peas are climbers. Many people love sweet peas and some people call them the "queen of one-year flowers."

In the winter the roots of the sweet pea plants die. If some seeds have fallen, new plants will start to grow in the spring. But not everything about the sweet pea is sweet. If you see a seed, do not eat it. It is full of poison and you may get sick.

The Immigrants

Between 1820 and 1920 many people moved to America. Some came to find better jobs. Others came because they were not free in their own lands. Others came because their country's leaders did not like them. Most people just came looking for a better life. They were called immigrants.

Most of these people came to America on sailing ships. Some trips took only a few weeks. Others took months. Some people could afford a cabin for themselves. They were lucky. The rest stayed in large rooms below the deck. The rooms were crowded and often dirty. The food was very poor. The water was sometimes rough. The trip was very dangerous.

The immigrants finally arrived in New York. Then they would wait in line for hours. They had to find out if they were healthy enough to stay. There was a long line for most people. There was a short line for richer people.

Many of these new Americans were not welcome. They could not speak English. They were different and strange. They were willing to work for low wages. But some factory owners would not hire them at all. These owners all seemed to forget one thing. Almost everyone in America had family members who were immigrants themselves.

Child Slaves

Everyone knows that slavery is wrong. But slavery is still very common. And one of its worst forms is child slavery. Poor families are the most likely victims. Farm owners can make families pay for their food and shelter. The family can not earn enough to pay the owners back. So everyone in the family works to try to pay the debt. Most of the time, they will never succeed. But the owners don't care! All those years of cheap work are too valuable.

Often the parents can no longer work. But the children must still work for the owners. The children can not go to school. They can never stop working to pay what they owe. Some owners are at least kind to the children. Then their life is a little better. But other owners are cruel. Children may not get enough food to stay healthy. If the child misses a day of work, the family must pay a fine. Then they will owe even more.

Many countries have laws against children working. But no one in the family knows about the laws. They don't know that their children have rights. And so it is very difficult to stop people from using children as slaves.

How Banks Work

Some people save their money by putting it in a bank. The bank pays them for this money. The money that the bank pays is called interest. People can earn about fifteen dollars every year for saving five hundred dollars in the bank. Why would a bank pay people for keeping their money in the bank?

Other people borrow money from the bank. They want to buy things that they need but they do not have the money. They ask the bank to lend them the money. But the money is not free. The people must pay to use it. This means that the people have to pay back all the money that they borrowed. Then they have to pay the bank for letting them use the money. They may have to pay the bank fifty dollars to borrow your five hundred dollars for one year. This is how the bank makes money.

People who save money in a bank earn interest. People who borrow from the bank must pay. Maybe Benjamin Franklin was thinking about that when he said, "A penny saved is a penny earned."

Frida Kahlo

Frida Kahlo was born in Mexico in 1907. She was an intelligent and beautiful young woman. She planned to become a doctor. But when she was 18 years old, she was in a bus accident. The accident broke her back in three places. After a long time in the hospital, she had to stay in bed for months. To pass the time, Frida began to paint. She soon found her talent and her love.

Some of her friends saw that Frida's paintings were very interesting. They helped her to meet Diego Rivera, a famous Mexican painter. Diego helped Frida to develop as a painter. They soon fell in love and married. But their marriage was troubled and painful. Frida soon learned that painting helped her to deal with her feelings. She painted many pictures of herself. She often said that she was the subject she knew best of all.

Frida had many operations on her back. Her great pain and her great strength made their way into her paintings. She had a rare ability to express pain and unhappiness through art. For this reason Frida Kahlo is seen as one of the truly great talents of her time. A museum in Mexico shows only her works. She is one of very few women artists who have ever achieved that honor.

Krakatoa

(crack-uh-toe-uh)

Krakatoa was a small island volcano about five miles wide. Over many years it had grown bigger from dozens of small eruptions and lava flows. That was before the morning of August 27, 1883. At the end of that day there was almost no island left. The volcano had exploded. Almost three quarters of the island was gone. Much of it was blown miles into the sky. The dust in the air shaded the sun for months.

It was lucky that no people lived on the island. But there were many islands close by where people did live. The huge waves caused by the blast killed many people. Some waves were as high as twelve-story buildings. They washed whole villages into the sea. Almost 36,000 people died.

The explosion of Krakatoa was heard 2,800 miles away. Windows in homes 100 miles away were broken. Many people think that the explosion was the biggest that ever happened on earth. Over the years a new volcano has risen. It is very close to the old island. Some people believe that it took Krakatoa's place. It has been named "Child of Krakatoa." Many people have read about that first great explosion. Some of them believe that we may not have heard the last of Krakatoa after all.

Sugar Gliders

Would you want a pet that thinks you are a tree? Then the sugar glider is the pet for you. Sugar gliders are members of the possum family. They are about the size of small flying squirrels and they have arms and legs shaped like bat wings. In the wild they spend their days huddled in their tree nests. They use their wings to glide from branch to branch in their tree without ever touching the ground. In the early evening they look for food and protect their special tree.

They make perfect pets because they enjoy being near their owner's body, sitting on a shoulder or on top of the head or cuddled inside a shirt pocket. To train the baby sugar glider you must wear two T-shirts and put the baby between them. Then you try to forget it is there and go about your regular life. It will explore its new home and the claws on its tiny toes will tickle you. It will take two weeks to train the sugar glider to accept you as its new home. Once that happens, it will always treat you as its own "tree." If you leave your pet in another room, it will glide back to you as soon as it sees you.

Sugar gliders like to eat sweet fruits. But bananas make them sick. Without lots of water, sugar gliders will die, so they must learn to drink from a water bottle. A pet sugar glider can live for 10 to 15 years.

The Mosquito

The next time you smack a mosquito on your arm and say to yourself "Got him!" you should think again. Actually, you got *her*! Only the female mosquito does the biting. She is in search of fresh blood to feed the eggs that will soon become more little Draculas. The female mosquito finds her victims by following streams of carbon dioxide. This is the gas that is exhaled by the warm-blooded animals she seeks. The carbon dioxide guides the mosquito to her prey.

Once she has found you, she is hard to stop. Unless you hear the telltale buzzing of her wings, you will probably never know she is there. She lands very lightly on her feet. Once she has landed she inserts her long, needle-like nose into your skin. Her nose is so thin that most people never feel the needle at all. Before she can start sipping your blood, she injects a little saliva to make it thinner. Otherwise it is like trying to drink a thick milk shake through a straw. It is the saliva that the mosquito leaves behind that makes the skin itch and swell.

Some people are lucky enough to feel her and fast enough to smack her. She may leave a smear of blood on their bare arm. But they weren't fast enough. That blood they see is their own! It is no surprise that mosquitoes are not the most popular of insects, unless you happen to be a spider or a bat! In addition to being pests, they also carry and spread diseases like malaria and the West Nile virus. But until we think of a better way to control them, mosquitoes will continue to annoy any animal that has blood and thin skin.

Oil Spill

On the night of March 24, 1989, a huge oil tanker named the *Exxon Valdez* ran into a reef in Prince William Sound in Alaska. It was carrying oil from the Alaska Pipeline to the mainland U.S. More than 11 million gallons of crude oil spilled from the ship. This was the largest oil spill in U.S. history. The spill was a terrible shock to the residents and Coast Guard that night. They did not know that the spill would soon get much worse.

At first, the Coast Guard tried to burn up the oil. But bad weather made controlled burning difficult. Then cleanup crews tried to scoop the oil from the water. But their equipment quickly became clogged with seaweed and thick oil. To make matters even worse, the spill site could be reached only by boat or helicopter. Crews sent to help clean oil-coated animals were slow to arrive. Then they just could not work fast enough. There were too many birds and animals that needed to be cleaned. The oil spill is estimated to have killed 250,000 sea birds, including 250 bald eagles. Nearly 3,000 sea otters and 22 killer whales were lost in the spill as well.

All in all, 140 miles of coastline were soaked with oil. Nearly 1,500 miles had some oil. Exxon Corporation has spent an estimated 2.5 billion dollars in the clean up of the spill. The fishing industry in Alaska is still not the same. Many fishermen feel that it never will be. Experts predict that the effects of the spill will be felt for decades to come.

Bullying

Most people experience bullying at some point in their lives. Bullying includes name-calling, making up harmful stories, shoving, or punching. Bullies tease people about how they look, act, or speak. They may even spread rumors and send insults by e-mail.

When you are bullied, you may feel sad and afraid to go to school. Some victims have even turned to violence to get revenge. The murders and suicides at Columbine High School in 1999 are examples.

Sometimes even your friends may not want to help. They are afraid that they will become victims too, but they often feel guilty for not helping.

While it is hard to know what to do, you should tell someone you trust like a parent, coach, or teacher. The important thing is to tell someone who is wise enough to help without making the situation even worse.

At school, try to stay away from the bully. On the bus, change your seat to be near the driver. At lunchtime, look for groups of people you know and try not to sit alone. Whatever you do, always think about your actions. Try to act confident and try not to act upset even though you may feel that way.

It is important to understand that bullies need help, too. They don't often understand the reasons for their actions. Bullies are often in trouble. About 40% of bullies have three or more arrests by age 30. They seldom think about the effects of what they do to others. That is why punishing bullies does not often help. Psychologists have found that bullies have often been victims of abuse during their lives. Bullies must learn that their actions can not be allowed. But remember that in every case of bullying, there are usually two people who need help.

A Community of Wolves

Wolves are probably one of the most misunderstood animals on our planet. Many myths and legends depict wolves as tricky, cunning, and dangerous. Who doesn't remember "The Big Bad Wolf" and "Little Red Riding Hood" or the "Werewolf" legend? This image, however, couldn't be further from the truth. Wolves may be dangerous . . . to rabbits, deer, pigs, sheep, and cattle. But you don't have to worry that one will eat you or your granny up!

Actually, wolves are part of a closely knit family that consists of 2 to 10 adults and any young pups. All of the wolves in the pack share responsibility for the young. The wolves travel in packs for the sake of more successful hunting, for mutual protection, and for companionship. Wolves are also territorial. They usually travel within a specific range, sometimes up to 50 square miles.

Many experts believe that it is the wolf's eerie howl that plays on the fears of humans. In fact, their howl is part of a sophisticated communication system within their group. Howling is the wolves' way of "staying in touch" over long distances. If a wolf is separated from her pack, she will begin howling. This is a cry for help as well as a call to reunite. It can, however, be very costly. If a competing pack is within her range, they may seek her out and kill her. Pups are especially vulnerable. They have not yet learned the appropriate times and places for howling.

Other purposes for howling include warning rival packs to keep moving or staking a claim on fresh-killed prey. The so-called *chorus howls* are used to make competing packs think that there are really more wolves in the pack. The next time you hear a wolf howl, you will know it is not a werewolf howling at the moon. Perhaps it is only a lost wolf looking for its pack.

Are You Afraid of Sharks?

Every summer in the United States, we hear about shark attacks. On some beaches, it is even common to see sharks swimming offshore. Other beaches will be closed because there are so many sharks swimming near the shore. But how likely is it that if you go for a dip in the ocean you will be attacked by a shark? Not very likely at all!

We are far more likely to be killed by another person than by a shark. Most scientists believe that the few shark attacks that occur are really mistakes. When we tan, the top portion of our foot turns brown while the bottom remains white. This shading is similar to that of many fish. Others think sharks mistake us for sea lions or seals, which are some of their favorite food. When they realize that they have made a mistake, most sharks simply spit out their victims and leave. Just think about it . . . if sharks wanted to have us for dinner on a regular basis, they could just come to any shore in the U.S. and help themselves.

Sharks should probably be more afraid of us than we are of them. The total shark population is in decline as a result of human hunting. For example, in some countries shark fin soup is a delicacy and the fins are very much in demand. The shark fin itself is often used in ceremonial dinners. When local fishermen capture the shark, they will use the entire body, but commercial fishermen have been known to follow the practice of *finning*. They cut off the fins of any sharks caught in their nets. They then throw the sharks back into the sea, leaving them to bleed to death. And *we're* afraid of *them*?

Since we do not have "shark farms" as we do for catfish or shrimp, constant fishing leads to overkilling of certain kinds of sharks. They simply cannot reproduce quickly enough to keep up with the demand. Although we may fear sharks with good cause, destroying them beyond rescue may be even more harmful to us all in the long run.

Squirrels

Watching squirrels can be a very entertaining pastime. To understand squirrels, you must remember that at heart they are concerned with three things: food, shelter, and mating.

Squirrels need one pound of food each week. They manage to balance their eating between immediate and future needs. Food is often in abundance during the late summer and early fall and so squirrels store food for later times when it may be scarce. They are successful at storing food because of their keen memory and good sense of smell. They leave a scent on the food that they bury, using sweat glands located between their foot pads and toes. The scent allows them to quickly locate food that they have hidden.

Squirrels mainly eat nuts, seeds, and fruit. They have sharp front teeth called incisors and powerful jaw muscles. These muscles help them gnaw hard food. Their incisors grow six inches each year. They chew on tree branches to keep their teeth clean, sharp, and short.

Squirrels eat heavily for several hours after sunrise and before sunset. Between feeding times, they usually rest in nests that change with the season. In the winter, large nests are located in a cavity in a tree trunk or on a branch lined with leaves and grasses. In the summer, squirrels stay in smaller ball-shaped nests made of plant materials. The adult squirrel usually lives alone; however, squirrels often share nests during very cold times. The nest is extremely important to the female since baby squirrels are dependent on her for nearly eight weeks. The nest is located high up in a tree, so life in the crowded space can be very dangerous for baby squirrels.

Parents mate during late winter and babies are born in the spring. The female wants to mate with the older and stronger males so she runs from the young males. Consequently, the squirrels' acrobatic skills are truly spectacular during mating time. They move quickly, jumping from tree to tree without falling. Their tails enable them to balance their bodies in motion.

Mary Jemison

Mary Jemison was born in 1743 on board a ship sailing to America. Her family settled in a rural community near what is now Gettysburg, Pennsylvania. Mary's father showed no fear of the reports of Indian raids that he heard from their neighbors. Her mother, however, had always felt differently. On April 5, 1758, her fears came true. A party of French soldiers and Indians raided the Jemison farm. Her terrified mother told Mary to obey her captors, remember her English language, and never forget who she was. Mary was taken away by her captors. Unknown to her, Mary's parents and most of the rest of her family were killed. Mary would have to rely only on her mother's words throughout the long days of captivity.

Mary was given to a pair of Seneca Indian women whose brother had been killed in battle. The women had a simple choice. They could kill Mary in revenge for their lost brother. Or they could adopt her to replace him. They chose to adopt Mary and treated her as their own sister, with a great deal of kindness. Mary missed her parents and family and at first could not be happy. She prayed and practiced her English language every day. But she eventually came to appreciate and respect her two new sisters. At the same time, she began to recognize the qualities that the Indian tribe demonstrated in their daily life. She characterized the Indians as extremely faithful to each other, very honest and honorable in all that they did. Mary married a Seneca warrior in 1765 and had several children of her own.

After the Revolutionary War, Mary was offered her freedom by the tribe. Her son was eager to see his mother go and live with her own people. Mary, however, could not bring herself to leave her son. She also worried about how she and her family would be treated by white people. She was afraid they might view her as a traitor. And so she chose to remain with her Indian family and spend the remainder of her days with them. Mary Jemison died in 1831, having spent more than 70 years as an Indian captive.

Selfish Survival

Throughout a queen bee's relatively short life, she has two essential jobs. The first job is secreting a chemical that spreads among all the worker bees, limiting their interests to nothing but work throughout their lives. The second job is laying eggs, and this task keeps her from having any time to even eat; consequently, she must be fed by a small group of worker bees.

How did this bee become the queen of a hive that contains nearly 20,000 bees? Her ascent to royalty started with a story of death and intrigue. The bee larvae are fed with a creamy white royal jelly that contains high levels of nutrients and acid. The strongest larva is selected as the queen and, once she is hatched, she goes on a murderous rampage, destroying all other potential rivals, hatched or not. To celebrate her victory, the new queen takes what is known as a mating flight. She flies to a large group of drones and while in flight, she mates several times. But in the bee world, the mayhem continues and as each drone mates with the queen, his abdomen is ripped open and he dies. The surviving drones are not welcome in a hive and they cannot feed themselves because their bodies cannot harvest nectar or pollen. They are structured solely for mating and do not even have a stinger. They have outlived their usefulness and die of starvation.

The queen has a pouch that she uses to store the sperm that she has collected and will use throughout her entire life to fertilize her eggs. Her task is made more comfortable by the efforts of dozens of worker bees that keep the hive cool by fanning their wings 11,400 times per minute!

But even the queen is not exempt from the rule of usefulness to the community. If she were to run out of sperm, she would lose her royal status and be replaced at once. One of the newly hatched female bees would be moved by the workers to a special cell. There she would be fed royal jelly while all other larvae are fed a mixture of honey and pollen. Eleven days later, she would hatch, the old queen would be ousted, and the process of survival would carry on.

Wayward Whales

Whales can be seen in very unexpected places. For example, a large Beluga whale was seen swimming up the Delaware River in Pennsylvania by some fishermen who couldn't believe their eyes. They saw the whale dive into the water, but it didn't reappear for quite some time. This was unusual because Beluga dives usually last only 3 to 5 minutes. Beluga whales, like other marine mammals, have a body structure that is designed for diving. When they dive their heart rate slows down from 100 to about 12 to 20 beats a minute and all of their bodily functions slow down with it.

Reporters from all over came to Pennsylvania to watch the whale. Belugas are easy to observe since they often swim in shallow water where their bodies are barely covered. And they usually swim slowly, about two or three miles per hour. However, if they need to, they can swim at thirteen miles an hour for as long as fifteen minutes.

People began to worry that the whale was lost and would die in the river. Belugas normally live in the Arctic Ocean and the seas that join it. They have a layer of blubber just beneath the skin. This blubber makes up forty percent of the whale's weight and keeps its body from losing heat.

The people in Pennsylvania should not have been that surprised since Belugas often go to rivers to look for food. In fact, Beluga mothers take their young calves to the warmer waters of the Churchill River in Canada. They can be found there from May to August gorging on capland, a small fish that is plentiful there. There are often 50 Belugas in a feeding group that make shallow dives and feast frantically on the capland. Tourists go out in small boats to watch their feeding frenzy. Belugas are also very vocal. They communicate by making high-pitched whistles, squeals, and even bell-like tones. They can find food by making sharp clicking sounds and interpreting the echo they recover. Belugas are often called *sea canaries* because of the chirping sounds they make, but certainly not because of their size!

The whale in the Delaware River finally left. No one, even the scientists, ever really understood why it came there in the first place.

Dams

Do you ever smile when you hear people talking about "water shortages"? After all, more than three quarters of the earth's surface is covered with water! The problem, however, is more complex than it seems. Only one fortieth of the world's water is fresh water and less than one third of that exists in fluid form. And as the population grows and cities expand and demand for water increases, people are faced with difficult decisions at every turn.

One solution that has been used throughout the world in rapidly increasing numbers is dams. Dams can convert even modest streams of water into a source of electrical power. They can be used to store water for human consumption or crop irrigation, cooling or transportation. They can even provide recreation on the artificial lakes that are created as a result of dams. Many major cities throughout the world are completely dependent on dams as a source of water. Dams have become an integral part of the successful settlement of the world's population. In fact, they affect, in one way or another, nearly every human being on earth.

But dams are not an unmixed blessing. For nearly every artificial lake we create, there are people and animals that must lose their land and sometimes even their homes. Water stored in artificial reservoirs evaporates more rapidly than water left in its natural state. Many species of fish that migrate to their spawning grounds have suddenly found their way blocked by the creation of dams. And when a dam fails, the loss of life and property can be catastrophic. For all of these reasons and many more, public opposition to the construction of dams can be fierce.

Engineers have developed ingenious ways to overcome some problems, such as building ladders to help migrating fish find their way to the tops of dams. Some problems, of course, can never be overcome. And so the proponents and the opponents of dams fight on. Even the United Nations has tried to ease the tensions between groups. In 2001, it appointed an international commission to share information about the costs and benefits of dams. The commission tries to help countries plan more effectively in the construction of new dams and the removal of unnecessary ones. But with no solution in sight for the world's water demands, the groups must learn to disagree without losing respect for one another's point of view.

Jane Addams

Jane Addams was born in Cedarville, Illinois, in 1860, just before the start of the Civil War. She grew up in a trying time in America, but spent her youth in a tranquil, privileged home. Jane dreamed of going away to a "real" college, like Smith College in Massachusetts, but she never had that opportunity. Instead, she complied with the wishes of her family and attended a local college, Rockford Female Seminary. But Jane's disappointment was short-lived. At Rockford she met a girl who would become her lifelong friend and co-worker, Ellen Starr.

Jane and Ellen shared a deep concern for the problems experienced by immigrants to the United States. Together they founded a social settlement called Hull House, on Chicago's West Side. Hull House served the needs of immigrants from many nations and of many colors. Jane and her co-workers offered child care, clubs, activities, and citizenship classes. They even provided an employment service as well as music and art activities. These were designed to help immigrants value and celebrate their own heritage. Hull House was also a much-needed safe meeting place for the new trade and labor unions. But above all, it was a place where immigrants could find help in learning about American ways.

Jane Addams became one of the most influential American women of her time. Her work extended far beyond Chicago and Hull House. She became part of the national and international reform movement for social justice. Jane helped establish the first juvenile court and helped develop the first legislation to protect women and children from abuse. Jane was also part of the creation of the Federal Children's Bureau in 1912 and the first child labor laws in 1916.

Jane was the first president of the National Conference for Social Work. She was among the founders of the National Association for the Advancement of Colored People in 1909. She played the same role for the American Civil Liberties Union in 1920. Both of these groups are still active today.

Jane Addams was part of an international group of women who opposed World War I and fought for peace and freedom. Jane received worldwide recognition. She was awarded the Nobel Peace Prize in 1931. She was the first American woman to receive it.

She may never have achieved her goal of going away to college. Yet, Jane Addams made the world a better place!

Possums

The possum, sometimes called North America's kangaroo, is its only marsupial animal. A female possum gives birth to over 20 babies, each no bigger than a honeybee. Only the first thirteen that crawl their way to the mother's pouch and attach themselves to one of her available nipples will survive. They remain in the pouch for 3 months and then crawl out and cling to the mother's fur. When they become too heavy to hold on, they fall off to the ground. At that time they are fully weaned and can begin their own search for food and shelter.

The study of possum habits shows that they do not need a permanent home. They usually spend only 2 or 3 days in another animal's hideout. Then they leave to find another. Their paws are too soft to dig holes to live in, but they seem to adapt anywhere they find the food, water, and shelter they need. Possums do not hibernate but they find winter very challenging. Their tails are particularly prone to frostbite since they have no fur covering. As a result, they often change their nocturnal habits in winter and eat during the day when it is warmer. The possum is very docile and, in addition to its many natural predators in the wild, humans, cats, and cars take their toll on possums. In fact, most possums never reach adulthood, living only 1 to 2 years.

Trappers who hoped to establish a fur industry brought the possum to New Zealand. At the height of the fur trade, 20 million possums were trapped yearly. However, the possum, with no natural enemies in New Zealand, quickly became a national pest. It loved the juicy new growth on several native trees. And because it returns to the same tree night after night until the leaves are gone, the destruction to vegetation was unbelievable. Seventy million possums nightly destroy 20 tons of growth, or the equivalent of 190 million hamburgers.

In spite of the deep resentment felt for possums in New Zealand, residents in several counties in Florida pay tribute to them. During the Depression, when little food was available, people survived because of the abundance of possum. The residents of Chipley, Florida, show their appreciation through their yearly celebration of the Possum Festival.

Insect Camouflage

When it comes to adapting to life on earth, there may be no species that does it better than the insect. If you are tempted to think that humans are at the top of the list, it may be time to reconsider. It is estimated that for every person on the face of the earth, there are one million insects and, if taken together, they would outweigh us by about 12 to 1. And their sheer ability to adapt to their surroundings makes them arguably the most successful creatures alive.

Take, for example, insect larvae. Unlike primitive insects whose young resemble the adults into which they will grow, more complex insects go through radically different stages of development. Grubs turn into beetles, maggots develop into flies, and caterpillars morph into butterflies. But the very complexity of their development presents some monumental problems. Unlike the insect that they will soon become, larvae have none of the traditional means of escaping predators; they are not built to move or flee; they are built only to eat and grow. Their lack of mobility is of little consequence to grubs and maggots; they do their eating out of sight of the world. Caterpillars, however, are a different matter since their banquet table is in the woods, in full view of dozens of hungry potential predators. How then can they ever win the perpetual battle to be a diner rather than a dinner?

The answer is quite simple: Caterpillars are among the greatest camouflage artists the world has ever seen. For example, the larvae of geometer moths have taken on the size and shape of tree twigs and are virtually undetectable while feeding on leaves. The Tiger Swallowtail larvae look remarkably like fresh bird droppings on a leaf, effectively discouraging predators from even considering them as food. Some caterpillars have eye-like markings on the side of their head. When disturbed by a hungry bird, they weave from side to side, mimicking a dangerous tree snake.

Other caterpillars use equally ingenious escape mechanisms. When detected, the Looper caterpillar will jump off the branch where it is feeding and its predator will search futilely for it on the ground below. But the Looper is really an accomplished bungee jumper who watches the search below while hanging from the branch by a thread of silk.

We have just scratched the surface of the enormous array of survival techniques used by insects. It may be that when it comes to sheer problem-solving and adaptability, humans, especially soldiers, may have much to learn from the lowly insect.

Old Man River

For many midwestern Americans living along the floodplains of the Mississippi River, the Great River was the source of their livelihood. The commercial traffic that flowed daily on the river provided goods and employment for thousands of people. But as William Faulkner wrote, the river was like a mule that would work for you for ten years just for the privilege of kicking you once.

And one of the river's hardest kicks was delivered in 1993 when a huge flood caused widespread destruction, leaving nearly 75,000 people without homes in nine states. The flood caused over 15 billion dollars in damage. To be sure, the Mississippi had flooded before and old-timers in the town could remember many flood years in their lifetimes. But 1993 seemed to almost everyone to be the worst of them all. This flood broke high-water records all across the Midwest. But to the people living along the floodplains, the Great Flood of 1993 was simply another of life's challenges to be met and overcome. They would rebuild their homes with help from the Federal Emergency Management Agency (FEMA). After the inconveniences and obstacles had been overcome, life would go on just as it had so many times in the past.

But no one could foresee that this time things were different. The U.S. Congress was apparently tired of flood emergency claims year after year and so instead, it announced a grand social experiment. It would no longer help the citizens living on floodplains to rebuild their homes in the same place. Congress instructed FEMA to help them rebuild their homes and towns in locations that were not as prone to flooding. In 1993 alone, over 10,000 homes were relocated but hardships, as always, seemed to relocate along with the homes. Many citizens complained that their new homes, built on more expensive land, drove up their mortgage debt. Others felt the loss of friends as towns and communities went their separate ways rather then relocating together.

But, as is so often the case, there were also many success stories. Many towns managed to stay intact and to plan newer and better communities. Many local leaders emerged to help their friends and fellow townspeople ease the stresses of the drastic changes in their lives. It is too early to tell whether the experiment has worked for the greater good of all, but one certainty has emerged from the flood of 1993. The U.S. Congress will probably never again help flood victims stay in the same places just to wait for the next great flood to strike.

The Wise Woman Doctor

Many people characterize medieval Europe almost exclusively as the Dark Ages. Historians, on the other hand, know that there were many bright spots. And one of the brightest was the medical center at Salerno in southern Italy. This center had earned a worldwide reputation as the home of the first formal medical school. Contrary to all social customs, women studied and learned here side-by-side with men, using Greek, Arabic, and Jewish texts. One of these women was Trotula di Ruggerio, known more affectionately as the "wise woman teacher." Trotula's primary interest was attempting to lessen women's suffering. She did this by listening closely to what her patients had to say about their ailments. She believed that it was the doctor's responsibility to ensure the comfort of patients and to foster healing. Some practices she recommended included warm herbal baths, diets, and massages. She also advocated plenty of rest to foster positive attitudes. Not only were Trotula's practices innovative for her times, but her views challenged some very central social assumptions. For example, she believed that problems with fertility could be caused by the male, not just the female, as was commonly believed.

Trotula is widely credited for having written key textbooks used during her life and for many years after her death. Her most notable work, *The Diseases of Women*, was written for male students, since information about the female body was not widely known. In many ways, Trotula was ahead of her time, especially her use of drugs to lessen the pain of childbirth. This practice illustrates her willingness to challenge the predominant religious views of her time. The Church held that women were destined by God to suffer during childbirth.

She is credited with performing life-saving surgeries for both infants and mothers during childbirth. Her books are recognized as pioneering two fields of study, obstetrics and gynecology.

It would be wonderful to report that the social gains and opportunities for education at Salerno continued for many years to come. Unfortunately, in 1194 King Henry VI destroyed the medical school at Salerno. From that point on, women were not permitted to study medicine. In fact, they were deprived of any type of education. Those women who continued practicing healing skills through the use of herbs and oils were often persecuted as witches. Many of Trotula's books were lost and some of her works were credited to male physicians. But most historians today accept Trotula as the author of these medical books because of the openness and frankness with which she wrote.

A Cold Case

On television shows about cold cases, detectives always seem to solve the mystery within the show's one hour time limit, but this is a far cry from reality. Actually, some of history's most infamous cases have never been solved at all. Jack the Ripper was never caught and the Boston Strangler case was never officially closed, even though a man confessed to the crimes.

The real job of cold case crime solving is often tedious, detailed work. It involves careful analysis of physical evidence from the crime scene with thorough investigative interviewing techniques. Technology including the Automated Fingerprint Identification System, along with DNA and chemical analysis, can help. Their results may not tell the police who the criminal was, but they may lead detectives to the elimination of possible suspects and witnesses. After extensive background checks and interviews, suspects and witnesses eventually may implicate the perpetrator.

A prime example of a case that combined all of these techniques is that of Robert Spangler, a convicted serial killer who had evaded justice for years. In 1978, neighbors discovered a 45-year-old woman, her 17-year-old son, and her 15-year-old daughter dead from apparent gunshot wounds. A suicide note was found by the mother's body. Police who interviewed the father, Robert Spangler, found gunshot residue on his hands. Even with two questionable polygraph tests, this was not enough evidence to charge him with murder since it is imperative that police provide credible evidence for an indictment. But with no statute of limitations on murder, time is on the side of the legal system. Tests that were not available to police at the time of a murder can be used on the physical evidence that still exists.

In 1993, 15 years later, Spangler married for the third time. While on a hiking trip in the Grand Canyon, he reported that his wife was missing. Park rangers later found her body, and classified her death as an accidental fall. Unknown to Spangler, they were very suspicious.

The park rangers requested help from local police and the Federal Bureau of Investigation (FBI). Because there was limited physical evidence, the FBI focused on interviewing techniques and background information analysis. Finally, agents interviewed Spangler and confronted him with their belief that he was a unique murderer. Spangler, suffering from terminal cancer, confessed to killing his first wife, his two children, and his third wife.

For more than 20 years after his first murder, Spangler was a free man. During that time he took at least one more life. Slow but thorough detective work coordinated at the local and federal level eventually led to his arrest and conviction. About 35 to 40% of homicides go cold in any given year. When they are solved, it is often through long, complex investigation and that kind of work is never completed in one hour!

The Author of Narnia

Many people are surprised that one of the world's most beloved writers of children's literature was actually very uncomfortable around children. And in reality, the life of C. S. Lewis included many such contradictions. Although Lewis was born in Ireland, he received most of his education in private boarding schools in England. He served England in World War I on the front lines in France, despite the fact that as an Irish national, he could have been exempted from service.

Lewis began his professional career as a tutor at Oxford University, surrounded by world-renowned scholars. He immediately began to fulfill his life's ambitions of becoming an author and scholar. By all accounts he was wildly successful in both areas. He wrote a series of children's stories which he called *The Chronicles of Narnia*. He also wrote science fiction novels for adults, and books about faith and belief. Many of his books became extraordinarily popular all over the world, a sticking point for some of his Oxford colleagues. By 1947, Lewis was famous enough to appear on the cover of *Time* magazine. And in 1956, Lewis published a study of 16th-century literature that to this very day is considered the definitive work on the subject. Yet Lewis never reached another of his major dreams, an appointment as a full professor at Oxford.

A lifelong bachelor, Lewis began correspondence with an American woman named Joy Davidman who often questioned him about ideas in his books. Lewis found that he enjoyed these challenging intellectual matches. Joy later took up residence in England but because of her involvement with the communist movement during her youth, she was threatened with deportation. Lewis went through a legal marriage ceremony to enable Joy to remain in England. Lewis and Joy did not live together but maintained their deep friendship. But when Joy was diagnosed with terminal cancer, Lewis realized something more. He was in love and wanted a real church wedding. They spent more than three delightful years living together after a near-miraculous remission of her cancer. When Joy at last succumbed to the disease, Lewis penned a journal that was later published as *A Grief Observed*. This book is a meditation on the mystery of life and triumph over sorrow that has served as a source of comfort to millions of readers.

Nine years before his death, C. S. Lewis was finally offered the post that had eluded him throughout his professional life, the position of full professor. But it was

Oxford's historical rival, the University of Cambridge, that made the offer. Faced with the prospect of losing one of its most distinguished and famous faculty members, Oxford quickly replicated Cambridge's offer. It was too little too late. Lewis happily spent the remainder of his career as a professor of medieval literature at Cambridge University.

Colored Snow

If you were hiking on the alpine slopes of the Sierra Nevada Mountains in California, you might come upon patches of pink snow with red streaks. If you walked on these patches of snow, the soles of your shoes would turn bright red and the cuffs of your pants would turn pink. For years this mysterious pink snow was a puzzle to mountain climbers and naturalists alike. In May 1818, Captain John Ross, traveling off the northwestern coast of Greenland, noticed white cliffs that were streaked with what looked like crimson blood. A report of his finding, published in the *London Times,* caused some readers to conclude that the red color was rust from a meteoric iron deposit. It was not until the end of the 19th century that this colored snow was recognized to be "blooms" of microscopic algae, or snow algae.

During the winter months snow algae are dormant. They do not begin germination until spring thawing when the nutrients in the melting snow reach them. This germination results in the releasing of smaller swimming cells that find their way to the surface. Researchers are not certain if the dissolved nutrients from the melting snow cause the cells to move to the surface. Some speculate that it has to do with the length of daylight and light density. The spores of the algae have thick walls and fatty deposits that enable them to withstand both the extreme cold temperature of winter and the high summer temperatures that would kill regular vegetative cells. The cells of some algae secrete mucilage that enables them to stick to one another and prevents them from being washed away.

Since the atmosphere is thinner in the higher altitudes, snow algae are exposed to damaging ultraviolet radiation. How can a plant thrive in such a severely cold environment with such bright light and high ultraviolet radiation? The cells of the snow algae contain carotenoid, a bright red pigment. This carotenoid serves as protection from the intense solar radiation at the surface of the mountain snow. The carotenoid is similar to that found in tomatoes, red peppers, carrots, and avocados. While carotenoids are widely used for food coloring, certain types have been found to possess cancer-fighting properties and some scientists believe that they have the potential to reduce risks of heart disease and eye degeneration.

Scientists have also discovered that a compound in grape skins inhibits clogging of the arteries; some scientists are hoping that the antioxidants produced by snow algae can have the same effect. It is clear that this once-confusing phenomenon has become a source of hope for researchers interested in finding cures for life-threatening diseases.

The Hawaiian Volcano

If you asked a hundred people where to find the most magnificent and tranquil tropical paradise on earth, it is a good bet that many would name the Hawaiian Islands. Few of them, however, would realize the extent to which the islands are a product of the pure, raw violence of nature. Incessant volcanic activity over a period of hundreds of thousands of years actually created the islands where no land had been before. A hot spot of magma (fluid rock material) thrust lava through the ocean floor to create a seamount, an undersea volcano. As the lava was cooled by the ocean water, it formed a massive mountain whose tip finally emerged from the sea. Mauna Loa, the most famous of the four active volcanoes in the Hawaiian chain, is really the world's highest mountain. If measured from the ocean floor to its summit, it towers 56,000 feet, dwarfing its more renowned brother, Mount Everest.

The lava flows from the volcano known as Kilauea began in 1983 and continue to this very day. Eventually, the lava reaches the cliffs and flows into the ocean below, where it hardens and adds yet more land to the Hawaiian Islands. Sometimes the cooled lava forms what is called a bench, an outcropping of hardened lava that is nonetheless very unstable. In fact, about 45 acres of such benches recently collapsed into the Pacific, adding yet more volume to the Big Island's coast. But before the real estate agents celebrate and the tourists flock to the newly created swimmer's paradise, they may need to remember the ferocity of nature in the islands.

The chemical reaction caused by the heat, chloride, and oxygen produces vast quantities of hydrochloric acid that can irritate the skin, and the superheated water that results from contact with the lava can cause third-degree burns. It will be many years after Kilauea ceases to erupt before anyone will be able to take advantage of the creative generosity of nature in that part of Hawaii.

You can visit both Mauna Loa and Kilauea at Volcanoes National Park and observe firsthand the creative work of Kilauea. There you can even walk on newly hardened lava, but be sure to wear tough shoes with thick soles. Much of the lava is rough and jagged with sharp edges, and there is also shiny, smooth lava that can crumble with the lightest pressure; in other words, don't walk there!

Some intrepid visitors can take a *doors off* helicopter ride for a bird's-eye view of the volcano and its surrounding lava fields. Vents of hot steam, molten lava, laze (lava haze), and vog (volcanic smog) are all part of the ride. Brace yourself to feel the heat and 120 mile per hour winds, and to see a stunning spectacle of lava emptying off the cliffs into the ocean below. You may even find yourself believing in the ancient goddess Pele who is said to live inside Kilauea and carry on her work of reshaping and recreating the Hawaiian Islands.

Politics and Friendship

There is an old saying that conflict can either deepen or destroy a friendship. Anyone tempted to doubt the truth of that maxim need only examine the relationship that existed between James Madison and Alexander Hamilton. Seldom have we encountered a more unlikely pair of friends. Madison was born to a wealthy family in Virginia, and received an education commensurate with his privilege. Hamilton was the child of an unwed mother and a father heavily in debt. But Hamilton possessed astounding skills and when, at the age of 15, he published an article, he stunned his readers with his proficiency in language. A group of wealthy readers decided to bankroll the fledgling writer and sent him to the American colonies for his first taste of formal education.

Madison began his distinguished political career at the age of 25 when he helped draft a new constitution for Virginia. It was then that Madison met Thomas Jefferson and their lifelong friendship began. Three years later, Madison's election to the Continental Congress afforded him the opportunity to promote his dream of a unified country, in contrast to a loosely confederated group of individual states.

In the meantime, Hamilton had embarked on a distinguished military career and when he too began his term of service with Congress, he met James Madison. The two men immediately recognized the congruity of their ideas, particularly the need for a strong federal government to guide the colonies.

Both Madison and Hamilton were named as delegates to the Annapolis Convention in 1786. It was there that the two most formidable intellectuals of their time cemented their relationship. Madison began to realize that Hamilton's passionate political style stood in sharp contrast to his own subtle style. Nonetheless, when Hamilton sought out his assistance in preparing the influential *Federalist Papers*, Madison rushed to his side. The *Papers* were a set of elegantly framed essays that succeeded in convincing New York's political leaders of the need for a strong federal government.

During George Washington's presidency, Hamilton became the country's first secretary of the treasury, charged with creating a plan for the payment of the nation's foreign debt. Hamilton proposed that all the new states pay equal portions of the war debt. The proposal generated much anger, but the strongest opposition to his plan came from none other than James Madison. Madison's home state of

Virginia had already paid much of its war debt and he believed that Hamilton's plan would punish those states that had acted responsibly.

Hamilton knew that he would need Virginia's support, but Madison refused to budge. Finally, Hamilton asked Thomas Jefferson, Madison's closest friend, for help. Jefferson promised his support on condition that the nation's capital would be located on the Potomac River, near his native Virginia. Hamilton agreed and his plan passed; however, he had paid a great price, both politically and personally. His longstanding relationship with Madison was now over. Madison went out of his way to avoid Hamilton for the rest of his life.

Context of Philosophies

In what ways do our personal experiences determine our views of the world? Consider the lives of two individuals with some common experiences but very different philosophies.

Antonio Gramsci was born in Italy in 1891. When he was six years old, the arrest of his father thrust the family into poverty. At the age of twenty, Gramsci was fortunate enough to obtain a scholarship to study at the University of Turin. Gramsci gradually became aware of Italy as a backward country controlled by corrupt politicians. He came to accept the socialist theory of Karl Marx. By the age of 24, he had become a forceful social, economic, and political critic. His revolutionary spirit was kindled by the success of the Bolshevik revolution in Russia. In an attempt to gain greater insight into communist theory, Gramsci moved to Moscow in 1921. But he was soon disillusioned by the terror and tyranny that characterized both Lenin and Stalin. When he returned home and found the same tactics used by Mussolini, his outspoken criticism resulted in his arrest. He was sentenced to prison in 1928. He spent the final nine years of his life writing about his socialist vision. He had come to believe that workers and peasants cannot bring about revolutions. He became an advocate of nonviolent socialist revolutions. He believed that these revolutions could be brought about only through an undermining of the values of the controlling majority.

Alexis de Tocqueville, on the other hand, was born in 1805 in Paris to an aristocratic family who had barely escaped the guillotine during the French Revolution of 1780. After a childhood haunted by fears of imprisonment, he was sent to college at the age of sixteen. He soon began to question the wisdom of the French aristocratic structure, even though his father held an influential position as a prefect. During the Revolution of 1830, his father lost that position and Tocqueville completely distanced himself from his aristocratic heritage. He believed that France was traveling a road toward internal revolution and destruction. Under the guise of studying the American penal system, Tocqueville requested permission to travel to the United States. His ultimate goal was to study democracy and his observations led to the publication of two volumes titled *Democracy in America*.

Tocqueville's interest in democracy continued when he returned to France. At the age of 39 he became part owner of a radical newspaper. Nonetheless, he remained opposed to Gramsci's kind of political agitation that could result in revolution. He tried to show his loyalty to France shortly before Napoleon's coup by helping restructure the government. However, Napoleon's distrust resulted in the overnight imprisonment he dreaded as well as a physical breakdown. In 1852, Tocqueville removed himself from political life and spent his final seven years writing. He had observed firsthand the great paradox of democracy. Without majority rule there can be no democracy, and once in power, the majority will always have the potential to tyrannize the minority.

Quasars

Ever since the dawn of humanity, searching the skies with more and more sophisticated instruments has led to a spate of new discoveries almost too breathtaking to keep up with. In the 1940s, for example, radio astronomers found that many celestial objects were emitting radio waves; most of these sources were common stars. But some faint blue-colored objects in the astronomical landscapes were very difficult to explain. They looked like stars but they emitted a huge quantity of very intense radio and ultraviolet waves, much more than could be expected from a typical star.

It was not until 1963 that Dr. Maarten Schmidt explained the phenomenon by examining the strange light spectrum emitted by one of the "stars." Schmidt deduced that the unusual red-shifted spectrum lines (the measure of an object's recession velocity) were part of a simple hydrogen spectrum. However, the only way that the objects could produce this type of spectrum was if they were traveling away from earth at a speed of almost 30,000 miles per second! And if that were correct, the objects would be more than 3 billion light years away, making them the most distant and, arguably, the most fascinating objects ever discovered in our universe. Because they were not true stars, scientists dubbed the strange objects quasars (for quasi-stellar radio sources).

Scientists were at a loss to explain how telescopes on earth could still detect such distant objects. To be detectable from earth, quasars would have to emit light as intense as that produced by 1,000 entire galaxies. In fact, the brightest quasar in the sky emits more than 2 trillion times the light of our sun, yet many quasars take up only about the space of our own solar system. Scientists today believe that the brightness of a quasar can be accounted for by the presence of super-sized black holes in the midst of huge galaxies. Black holes suck in passing stars and clouds of gas and, in doing so, heat huge quantities of matter to such an extent that they emit stupendous amounts of light. One amazing fact is that in order to create the light emitted by the brightest quasars in the sky, the black hole would have to consume as many as 10 stars the size of our sun every year.

Today scientists know of the existence of more than 60,000 quasars, with the most distant an astonishing 13 billion light years removed from earth. Because quasars are so distant, they must have been created in the very early stages of the development of the universe. Indeed, it would be logical to conclude that since it is taking billions of years for the light of some quasars to reach us, those quasars are no longer in existence. Only their light, still traveling over the vast expanses of the universe, is reaching us today. It is certainly true that quasars still raise more questions than scientists have answers for, but quasars are objects that unequivocally challenge the imagination of scientists and laypeople alike as we seek more and more answers to the mysteries of the universe.

The Search for Pancho Villa

America's hunt for the infamous Mexican revolutionary Pancho Villa in 1916 in reality was the result of a series of botched political, economic, and military decisions. The United States had huge business interests in Mexico, interests that were threatened by the Mexican Revolution of 1910. Anxious to protect these interests, President Woodrow Wilson decided to throw his support behind one of the leaders of the revolution, Venustiano Carranza, the Mexican president. Carranza was the man he believed to be most sympathetic to the American agenda. But Carranza regarded his American allies as something of a mixed blessing. While grateful for any support he could muster, Carranza remained fearful of alienating his own people by showing favor to the hated neighbor to the north. He refused to give in to some of Wilson's demands. In retaliation, Wilson then began to supply another revolutionary, Pancho Villa, with arms and supplies. It was Wilson's hope that Villa might overthrow Carranza and be more favorably inclined to the United States if he came into power.

But Villa's potential as a threat to the Mexican leader failed to materialize quickly enough to satisfy the American president. Wilson decided to make his peace with Carranza and recognize his government. Villa was infuriated at the desertion of Wilson and the loss of the support to which he had become accustomed. In retaliation, he and his men killed 16 Americans traveling on a train in Mexico. But his boldest attack occurred on American soil in the town of Columbus, New Mexico, and left 19 Americans dead. Villa hoped that by provoking a counterattack by the Americans, he could turn popular opinion against Carranza and expose his ties to the United States. Then Villa would be waiting in the wings to assume the leadership of all of Mexico.

America, in its turn, launched what came to be known as the Punitive Expedition against Villa and his men. Wilson sent General John J. Pershing and 5,000 soldiers, equipped with trucks, armored vehicles, and even airplanes, into Mexico to hunt down and destroy Villa and his army. Suddenly the overwhelming popularity that had never come about during all the years of Wilson's support materialized. Pershing naturally underestimated Villa's enormous support among the Mexican people. They consistently protected their local Robin Hood, giving Villa advance notice of Pershing's movements. They even supplied false information about Villa's whereabouts to Pershing's troops. After nearly two years of trying, Pershing had nothing to show for his efforts. He had not even come close to locating Villa. The Punitive Expedition was finally called off.

Despite the miserable failure of the expedition in achieving its primary end, many historians consider it a resounding success in the larger scheme of things. With the threat of World War I looming, American troops had the chance to familiarize themselves with their new weapons and technology. In particular, their use of reconnaissance aircraft, despite its failure in the short term, led to a great deal of success in the preparation for the war against Germany. John J. Pershing went on to become leader of the American forces in Europe and the most celebrated military leader of the war.

The Continent of Africa

Africa is a large continent made up of 54 countries. Many countries in Africa struggle with poverty, rebellions, famine, and disease while other countries have strong governments and economies with many resources.

Since 2003, the Darfur region of the country of Sudan has had continual strife between the Muslim government and rebel groups such as the Justice and Equality Movement and the Sudan Liberation Movement Army. Many of the tribal, civilian inhabitants of this region of Sudan have been massacred. Others live in encampments without fresh water and food, often separated from their families. A recent peace agreement holds out hope that this civil conflict will soon end; however, the International Committee of the Red Cross reports that the internally displaced people are still struggling to survive.

In the North Central African country of Niger, famine is wreaking havoc. Countless children are dying of malnutrition and disease and their distraught parents are helpless since they, too, are without food.

Robert Mugabe, the first and only president of Zimbabwe since it gained independence from Britain in April 1980, has become a tyrant. Mugabe has been burning makeshift homes and vegetable gardens in areas that did not support him in Zimbabwe's most recent election. Fuel and food shortages are also prevalent. In one of Zimbabwe's largest cities, Bulawayo, a loaf of bread costs 3,000 Zimbabwe dollars, or U.S. $3. But with most people earning the equivalent of only U.S. $18 per month, that is a huge sum of money. More than 70% of Zimbabweans are unemployed and the inflation rate is currently over 600%. Once considered the "breadbasket" of southern Africa, Zimbabwe has suffered tremendously because of the mismanagement of its current dictator.

Throughout the continent of Africa, various contagious diseases are widespread. Out of the 20 countries in the world with the highest HIV/AIDS rates, 19 of them are in Africa, mostly in the sub-Saharan areas. In addition to rampant malaria, common illnesses like polio, measles, cholera, typhoid fever, and diphtheria are still prevalent in Africa's population. The tragedy is that the vast majority of these diseases are preventable through vaccination. But in many African nations, vaccines and medicines that we take for granted are not even widely available.

Many organizations are working to combat the problems of famine, disease, and civil strife. However, as of yet, there is still much to do.

Some African nations are making significant progress toward prosperity and stability. In Botswana, another South African nation, agricultural and mining industries produce income to provide education and health care for their populace. Other countries have developed a strong ecotourism industry. These countries are helping protect natural wildlife and their habitats, while providing opportunities for both research and entertainment.

Many African nations have rich natural resources such as titanium, oil, diamonds, and other gems, along with minerals used in computers, cell phones, and medical equipment. Some countries, such as the Democratic Republic of the Congo, are fighting over them; others, such as Botswana, are utilizing them in responsible and controlled ways that support their economies and protect their supplies.

If it takes a village to raise a child, imagine what it will take to help countries in turmoil to prosper. Perhaps a careful examination of the countries that have succeeded on this vast African continent can help others to achieve the same successes.